The Ministry and Message of PAUL

Richard N. Longenecker

ZONDERVAN PUBLISHING HOUSE
OF THE ZONDERVAN CORPORATION
GRAND RAPIDS, MICHIGAN 49506

THE MINISTRY AND MESSAGE OF PAUL

Grand Rapids, Michigan

Eighth printing August 1976

Library of Congress Catalog Card Number 77-159661

Printed in the United States of America

TO OUR PARENTS

Mr. and Mrs. Carl Vogt Wilson

Mr. and Mrs. Ward F. Longenecker

Contents

Preface

This short introduction to the ministry and message of the apostle Paul is written with the beginning theological student, the working pastor and the alert Christian layman in mind. It comprises in the main two articles on "Paul the Apostle" and "Pauline Theology" originally written for the five-volume *The Zondervan Pictorial Bible Encyclopedia,* edited by Merrill C. Tenney and to be published by Zondervan Publishing House of Grand Rapids, Michigan. The manner of treatment, length of discussion and style reflect the controls exercised in that larger encyclopedia project, for the content of chapters two through nine corresponds exactly to that of the aforementioned articles. Chapters one and ten have been added that there might be a suitable introduction and conclusion.

I am indebted to Professor Tenney and the Zondervan Publishing House for the privilege of publishing this material separately in the "Contemporary Evangelical Perspectives" series, and to them I express my heartfelt thanks. It is my hope that in such a form the material will be more accessible to students and at the same time will commend *The Zondervan Pictorial Bible Encyclopedia* from which it is extracted.

RICHARD N. LONGENECKER

September, 1970

The Ministry and Message of PAUL

1

Introduction

The study of Paul's life and missionary activity is dependent to a great extent upon the narrative of the Acts of the Apostles. If the historicity of that account is rejected, scholarship is left to some process of divination or hypothetical reconstruction to determine the course of early church history. Paul, of course, furnishes additional information regarding events and their significance. And whenever possible, evidence drawn from his letters must be given priority by the historian, for the apostle was a participant in the matters which he relates. But even when available, the historical statements and allusions in the Pauline letters cannot supply an alternative outline to that of Acts. They presuppose a course of events, but they do not record a connected account of those events. For the message of Paul, on the other hand, the apostle's pastoral letters to his churches and to various individuals are of principal concern. Both the Acts of the Apostles and the canonical letters of Paul, however, have been subjects of extensive critical debate during the past two centuries, and therefore require some comment before turning directly to the ministry and message of Paul.

The Acts of the Apostles

The book of Acts, like the gospels, was written with a strong sense of the sacredness of the concrete facts which it narrates, since the author believed that the eternal purposes of God were fulfilled and revealed through what actually happened. That fact, of itself, does not, of course, relieve the author of the possibility of distorting the data in the interests of his thesis. Nor does it exonerate him from charges of omitting information which the modern historian may consider important, but which did not seem relevant for his purpose. It does suggest, however, that he has taken questions of facticity and accuracy seriously, and that before being set aside for a more modern construction, his account ought to be given a fair hearing.

The evangelist Luke claims for his gospel an accuracy of narration based upon eyewitness accounts (Luke 1:2-4), and there is reason to accept a similar intent for his narrative in Acts. Comparing Luke's gospel with that of Matthew (assuming a common use of Mark's gospel and a Logia source), it is possible more or less to check Luke's degree of variation from his sources. While there are obvious differences between the third and the first gospel due to differing interests, differing circumstances, and differing purposes, no charge of rank innovation can be laid against the writer of the third gospel. Similarly, no charge ought lightly to be entertained against his work in Acts, though there is no comparable "Matthew" by which to judge the handling of his materials there. Many today decry the "astonishing liberty" which they believe the author of Acts has taken in matters of facticity. But it must be said that the vast majority of their difficulties arise from their own lack of sympathetic listening to what Luke is trying to say, their own impatience with a selective writing of history, their imposition of modern criteria upon Acts in the writing of history, and the scarcity of contemporary first-century data which could validate more thoroughly the historical record of Acts.

Luke, it is true, varies considerably from the modern historian. In his work there is no citing of authorities, no striving for completeness, and no interaction with competing viewpoints. He presents his material in dramatic vignettes, which serve to present not so much a single picture as a series of glimpses. He is more interested in impressions than in the establishment of cause and effect nexuses. And what he does present often leaves his readers grasping for the unifying theme by which to integrate the whole (as witness the continuing debate on the purpose of Luke in writing). But although he has styled his presentation in a unique manner, is uninterested in some issues which preoccupy modern theological historiography, and is primarily concerned with proclaiming by means of history the continuing activity of the ascended Christ in His Church and the world, one is not obliged to relegate the narrative to the category of the historically unreliable. Evidently in Luke's view, only in such a manner could his history carry significance and be compelling.

Some scholars today prefer to deride the historical veracity of Acts on the basis of their understanding of what a kerygmatic witness ought to be or because their conceptions of the early church differ. But in so doing they verge perilously close to proceeding *per ignotum ad ignotius* in their portrayal of the apostolic days. It is noteworthy, as H. J. Cadbury once observed, "the extraordinary darkness which comes over us as students of history when rather abruptly this guide leaves us with Paul a prisoner in Rome." To discredit the history of Acts is to extend that darkness, not to illuminate. And if Acts deserves credence for its general outline, it must also be allowed due consideration when it comes to matters of detail; for the same qualities expressed in the one are present also in the other.

As to the speeches reported in Acts, a similarity of structure may be freely acknowledged without any necessary denigration of the authenticity of content. To an extent, all of the speeches of Acts are necessarily paraphrastic in their present form, for certainly the original delivery contained more detail of argument and more illustrative material than presently included — as poor Eutychus undoubtedly could testify (cf. Acts 20:7-12). Stenographic reports they are not. And probably few ever considered them as such. They have been restyled, as is true in every précis; and, furthermore, styled in accordance with the styling of the narrative. But the recognition of a styling which produces speeches compatible with the narrative in which they are found should not be interpreted as a necessary declaration of either inaccuracy of reporting or a lack of traditional material, since one author is responsible for the literary form of the whole.

In the third gospel, again by comparison with Matthew, Luke gives evidence of not inventing words for Jesus. On the contrary, he seems to have been more literally exact in the transmission of the sayings of Jesus than in the recording of the events of His life. Although it must not be pressed too far, such an observation provides a presumption in favor of a similar treatment in Luke's recording of the addresses of Peter, Stephen and Paul. And although his respect for the apostolic leaders never rivaled his adoration of Christ, it is difficult to believe that this difference would have greatly affected his historiographical methods or his desire for accuracy of reporting in the book of Acts as over against that in his gospel.

The Acts of the Apostles, then, presents itself in both its narrative and its speeches as an honest and informed attempt to relate certain crucial episodes in the advance of the Gospel during the apostolic days – particularly those episodes that set forth the advances culminating in the Pauline ministry. Despite the spate of recent criticism to the contrary, there is reason for the historian to use Acts with confidence. Therefore, in what follows, it will be so employed, though always testing and interpreting the data there given by reference to historical statements in Paul's own letters and with regard to what is known of the times from other historical sources.

The Letters of Paul

There is widespread agreement today that most, if not all, of the canonical missionary epistles of Paul and many of his canonical letters written from prison are authentic. Romans, First and Second Corinthians, and Galatians are so strongly attested both internally and externally that few have ever questioned them. First Thessalonians has been generally accepted, though the apocalyptic nature of the second letter to the Christians of Thessalonica has caused some at an earlier time to question Second Thessalonians. But with the realization that, though the apostle's eschatology was reoriented by his conversion to Jesus the Christ, it was not abandoned, the major argument against this epistle has been set aside. Colossians, Philemon and Philippians likewise have so commended themselves to scholars that none but the most radical have sought to oppose their authenticity, though questions have legitimately been raised regarding the exact locale for the composition of these letters.

The main current critical discussions as to Pauline authorship center on the letter to the Ephesians and the so-called Pastoral Epistles to Timothy and Titus. The rather general nature and style, the omission of the designation "in Ephesus" (Eph. 1:1) in the earliest extant manuscripts, and the striking similarity to Colossians have led many to view the letter to the Ephesians as a summary of and introduction to the other letters of Paul by a later disciple of the apostle. But while Ephesians is often considered the product of a post-apostolic Paulinist, the hypothesis that it was authored by Paul at the same time as the Colossian letter and that it was meant to be something of a circular letter to Christians in Asia Minor is at least as good an explanation for these peculiarities of style and structure as any other. Of the canonical letters claiming Pauline authorship, the most problematic are First and Second Timothy and Titus. These have been seriously questioned and discounted by many as being unauthentic, principally on the basis of their more formal tone and the high frequency of words not found elsewhere in the acknowledged writings of the apostle. But taking into consideration a difference of topic in these letters, the altered situation of the apostle at the time of writing, and the probable use of an amanuensis or secretary in the actual composition, such factors need not be viewed as fatal to Pauline authorship. Scholarship of late, in fact, has begun to realize that its criticism of the Pastorals has been extreme and is returning to a consideration of the authenticity of these three letters as a live possibility.

Many of the critical issues alluded to above will of necessity appear again in the discussion of Paul's ministry which follows. Let it suffice here to say that there are good reasons for accepting the thirteen letters of the New Testament which claim to have been written by Paul as being authentic, and this discussion of the ministry and message of Paul will in large part base itself upon them.

As for the anonymous letter to the Hebrews, the situation is more complex. While its theology and historical allusions are not incompatible with the Pauline message and ministry, its style of presentation and manner of quoting from the Old Testament are decidedly different from Paul's acknowledged writings. Alexandrian Christians early attributed its content to Paul in some manner, though they explained its present form by reference to either a disciple of the apostle or a translator. Elsewhere, however, Christians during the first four centuries seem to have been generally unconvinced, and only through the efforts of Jerome and Augustine was the letter widely accepted as from Paul. John Calvin had his doubts about the letter's Pauline authorship; and Martin Luther took it as a composition of Apollos, which suggestion is widely accepted today. Despite repeated attempts to solve the enigma and unravel relationships, Origen's early third century judgment regarding the work remains probably the sanest and best: "But as for myself, if I were to state my own opinion, I should say that the thoughts are the apostle's, but that the style and composition belong to one who called to mind the apostle's teachings and, as it were, made short notes of what his master said. If any church, therefore, holds this epistle as Paul's, let it be commended for this also. For not without reason have the men of old time handed it down as Paul's. But who wrote the epistle, in truth only God knows for sure" (Eusebius, Eccl. Hist. VI. 25. 13-14).

Other Historical Sources

The Roman historians, chiefly Tacitus and Suetonius, recount the circumstances prevailing during the first Christian century in the empire at large, and at times relate events that have particular bearing for Christianity within that empire. Josephus, the renegade Jew who wrote during the latter decades of the first century, is extremely important for a knowledge of events and circumstances in Palestine during the rise and early expansion of Christianity. Only occasionally, however, does he provide information directly related to the Christian faith itself, and seldom does he relate anything more about Judaism than the popular theology of the Jewish people whom he sought to defend. Likewise in the Talmud and its cognate codifications (literature representative of Pharisaic Judaism mainly after the fall of Jerusalem to the Romans) there can be found a few historical allusions which are of aid in reconstructing early Christianity during the first century. Mention must also be made of Hegesippus, a late second-century member of the Church of Aelia (Gentile Jerusalem), who is known to us in quotations from him by Eusebius and Epiphanius. From him we have knowledge of certain ecclesiastical traditions that were current in Palestine in his day, which, while obviously incorporating a degree of fanciful elaboration, preserve some genuine memories of the first-century Christians in that land. Also, of some significance are the Clementine Homilies (late second or early third centuries) and the Clementine Recognitions (first half of the fourth century), which purport to deal with the life of Clement of Rome: his early life, his contact with Peter, his missionary travels with Peter, and the final reunion of his family. In the guise of biography, their purpose was to communicate a gnosticizing Ebionite theology which was distinctly anti-Pauline. While very diverse evaluations of these works have been given in the past, there is a growing consensus today that they too offer some help in the reconstruction of events and thought during the first Christian century, even though quite indirectly.

2

The Man and the Pharisee

A Jew of the tribe of Benjamin (Phil. 3:5), Saul, "who is also called Paul" (Acts 13:9), was given the name of that tribe's most illustrious member – Israel's first king. His Hebrew name Saul means "asked for," while his Roman cognomen Paulos means "little."

Personal Details

Paul was born in Tarsus in the region of Cilicia (Acts 9:11; 21:39; 22:3). Little is known about his family directly. Jerome records a tradition which suggests that his parents originally came from a town in Galilee called Gischala, and that they fled to Tarsus during the Roman devastations of Palestine in the first century B.C. (Comm. on Philemon 23). Probably the home was fairly well-to-do, for if he were born a Roman citizen (Acts 16:37, 38; 22:25-29), his family must have possessed some wealth and standing. And from his rather self-conscious reference to "working with our own hands" in First Corinthians 4:12 and his somewhat awkwardly expressed word of thanks for a gift of money in Philippians 4:14-19, it may be surmised that he speaks as one whose natural place in society was quite the reverse of any proletarian status.

Jewish law prescribed that a boy begin the study of the Scriptures at five years of age and the study of the legal traditions at ten (Pirke Aboth 5:21). Josephus relates that both the Scriptures and the traditions were taught in every city to Jewish boys "from our first consciousness" (Contra Apion II. 18), and Philo speaks of such instruction "from earliest youth" (Leg. ad Gaium 210).

Undoubtedly Paul was immersed as a boy in such a curriculum as well, being taught in the synagogue school and at home. Jewish sentiment also asserted the nobility of manual labor, and advised that intellectual prowess and physical activity go hand in hand. Gamaliel II is credited with saying: "Excellent is Torah study together with worldly business, for all Torah without work must fail at length, and occasion iniquity" (Pirke Aboth 2:2). An early Jewish tractate insists: "Whosoever doth not teach his son work, teacheth him to rob" (BT Kiddushin 99a). Thus, Paul was also initiated into the skills of a tentmaker, which, while a rather menial occupation to the modern mind, was then probably considered a "clean and not laborious trade" (BT Berakoth 63a). Jewish education sought to produce a man who could both think and act; one who was neither an egghead nor a clod. And Paul's later life indicates that he profited greatly from such a schooling.

At thirteen a Jewish boy became a *bar mitzvah* ("son of the commandment"), at which time he took upon himself the full obligation of the Law and the more promising lads were directed into rabbinic schools under abler teachers. It was probably at this age, or shortly thereafter, that Paul came to Jerusalem to further his training, perhaps living with the married sister spoken of in Acts 23:16. Some have suggested that Acts 22:3 may more appropriately be punctuated as follows: "Brought up in this city [Jerusalem], at the feet of Gamaliel educated according to the strict manner of the law of our fathers"; this would allow for a residence in Jerusalem prior to this rabbinic training and would tend to discount Tarsian influence in his rearing. But while such a reading is possible, probably the better reading is: "Brought up in this city at the feet of Gamaliel, educated according to the strict manner of the law of our fathers" (as KJV and RSV); which directly associates his coming to Jerusalem with his rabbinic instruction. This latter reading has the advantage of allowing all the participles in verses three and four to begin their respective clauses uniformly. And it correlates well with Josephus' reminiscence of his own intensive Pharisaic instruction beginning "about fourteen years of age" (Life 2). It is some indication of Paul's youthful ability, and perhaps also of his parents' importance, that not only was he selected for further rabbinic study, but that he came to Jerusalem to study under one of the greatest Rabbis of the first century – Gamaliel I (Acts 22:3). And in the course of his studies, the young Jewish theolog came to excel over the majority of his contemporaries, becoming extremely zealous for the traditions of his fathers (Gal. 1:14).

As to his physical appearance, there are only indirect and rather allusive data from the New Testament. The fact that the residents of Lystra in their misdirected ardor identified Barnabas with Zeus, the chief of the Olympian gods, and Paul with Hermes, the winged messenger of the gods, possibly indicates the relative stature of the two missioners (Acts 14:12). Barnabas was probably the more stately and imposing figure, with Paul being inferior in physique, though more active of temperament. This suggestion of an unprepossessing appearance is borne out by the contemptuous remark of his antagonists at Corinth: "his letters are weighty and strong, but his bodily presence is weak" (II Cor. 10:10). Paul himself refers to two matters which must have marred his appearance to some extent, at least in later life: (1) a "bodily ailment," which he recognized as a trial to his converts and for which he prayed repeatedly for deliverance (Gal. 4:13-15; II Cor. 12:7-10); and (2) the "marks of Jesus" borne in his body, which probably means the marks of physical abuse suffered as a minister of the Gospel and which he viewed as sacred brands signifying his relation to his Lord (Gal. 6:17). In addition, the Corinthian letters offer evidence that Paul recognized his oratorical skills to be less than those of others (I Cor. 2:1-5; II Cor. 10:10; 11:6). Yet his letters also reveal a man of keen intellect, sensitive nature, infectious spirit, immense vitality, strong determination, and a vast capacity for friendship. A presbyter in the province of Asia during the second century described him as "a man small of stature, with a bald head and crooked legs, in a good state of body, with eyebrows meeting and nose somewhat hooked, full of friendliness; for now he appeared like a man, and now he had the face of an angel" (Acts of Paul and Thecla 3). While possibly only inferred from the New Testament data itself, this description may well rest upon genuine recollections from an earlier day.

It will probably never be conclusively settled whether Paul was ever married or not, though it seems most likely that he remained single throughout his life. The argument that as a member of the Sanhedrin (cf. Acts 26:10) he was required to be married and the father of children (BT Sanhedrin 36b) is not strong. This ruling, instituted in the interests of moderation in the face of rising zealot activity, dates from the time of Rabbi Akiba in the late first and early second centuries A.D. The necessity for its inauguration indicates that prior to this time such was not the case. Similarly, the view of Clement of Alexandria that Paul was really married, but left his wife at Philippi so that she would not interfere with his travels, and that he addresses her in the words "true yokefellow" of Philippians 4:3 (Stromata III.6), may be safely set aside. It would be incredible for Paul to urge the unmarried and the widows of Corinth to "remain single as I do" (I Cor. 7:8), if he had all the while been married. And that the Corinthian ascetics could point to him in substantiation of their views on continence suggests that he was unmarried rather than a widower.

Paul was distinctly a man of the city, with attitudes and experiences which prepared him to think broadly and minister widely. He had been raised in the thriving commercial and intellectual center of Tarsus and trained in the Israelite capital of Jerusalem; he concentrated his missionary activities on the great centers of Roman influence; and he looked forward to preaching in Rome, the capital of the empire. His urbanized outlook is seen in his metaphors, most of which are drawn from city life: the stadium (I Cor. 9:24-27; Phil. 3:14), the law-courts (Rom. 7:1-4; Gal. 3:15; 4:1, 2), the processions (II Cor. 2:14; Col. 2:15), and the market (II Cor. 1:22; 5:5). As one highly trained in the traditions of his fathers, who had also rubbed shoulders with Grecian culture and had inherited Roman citizenship, Paul was able to speak easily within every sector of the Roman world.

A Hebrew Born of Hebrews

To understand Paul aright, reference must be made to his life in Judaism; that is, first of all to his place and standing, and then to his activity and religious experience in the religion of his fathers.

Paul explicitly claims to be a Hebraic Jew trained in the most worthy traditions of his fathers, whose Pharisaic qualifications could hardly be surpassed (Phil. 3:5; II Cor. 11:22; Acts 22:3). Such a claim, however, has often been disputed; many consider it evident by the circumstances of his life in Tarsus and the attitudes expressed in his letters that Paul really belonged to the more liberal side of Judaism. The issue of itself is of little direct consequence, for certainly God is able to accomplish His purposes regardless of the background of the man He chooses. Yet the implications which may legitimately be drawn from either an orthodox Hebraic background or a more liberal Hellenistic orientation are of great importance.

In the first place, the claim that Christianity is the fulfillment of Israel's spiritual aspirations, as the apostle asserts, would be truly significant only if Paul were in a position to understand the deepest longings of the Old Testament and orthodox Judaism. Likewise, his attacks against the Judaism of his day would be meaningful only if he had been in a position to have known Judaism at its best. If his pre-Christian religious experience can be explained on non-biblical and non-Hebraic grounds, his lack of fulfillment in Judaism and his conversion to Christianity could be attributed primarily to Hellenism. One's attitude toward the validity of Paul's Hebraic claims therefore has great significance in one's evaluation of Paul's Christian polemic and doctrine, and for this reason the issue is vital.

While Paul has been frequently viewed as a "Hellenist of the Hellenists," many today have begun to take his Hebraic heritage more seriously. The old distinction between an orthodox homeland and a liberal Diaspora has not always held true, since the strength of Jewish orthodoxy varied not so much geographically as according to mental climate in a given community or home. Paul's understanding of the unity of the Law and his "pessimism" regarding man's ability to keep it can be paralleled in a number of passages in the Jewish literature of his day (e.g., Pirke Aboth 2:1; Mishnah Makkoth 3:14; BT Shabbath 70b; Tosephta Shebuot 3:6; IV Macc. 5:20, 21; 1QS 1.14; IV Ezra 7:116-126). His rehearsal of human inability as a backdrop for the supremacy of divine mercy and grace is distinctly in the tradition of the better Rabbis. Probably at no point does Paul reveal his orthodox training more than in his treatment of Scripture, where his usual practice is to reproduce the exegetical forms of the earlier teachers – not those of contemporary sectarian Judaism nor the excesses in atomistic treatment of the later Amoraim. And even his later Christian interest in Gentiles together with his doctrine of intimate personal union with God "in Christ," while differing in degree and content from Judaism because of his Christian perspective, have affinities with the nobler and loftier expressions in the Talmud. The deeper a person goes into the apostle's thought (allowing for differences effected by his risen Lord), the more one finds Paul's unquestioned assumptions, mental temper, and ways of expression to be rooted in the nobler Pharisaism of Judaism prior to the destruction of Jerusalem.

This is not to deny the presence of Grecian ideas and terms in his writings. Without betraying any profound influence of Hellenistic philosophy on his thinking, he can still (1) employ its religious language to expound Christian truth (e.g., Col. 1:15-20), (2) quote its authors (Acts 17:28; I Cor. 15:33; Titus 1:12), (3) argue theistically in similar fashion (Rom. 1:19, 20; 2:14, 15), and (4) use its diatribal form of presentation (e.g., Rom. 2:1 - 3:20; 9:1 - 11:36). These are matters which could have been acquired in his rabbinic study at Jerusalem, where prospective rabbis were taught something of the thinking of the Gentile world. Or they might have been gained in personal contact at Tarsus, or on his later missionary journeys. But however accumulated, they were employed by Paul because they could convey *his* meaning, without necessary reference to what they actually signified in Grecian religious philosophy. And they appear in his letters as features obviously secondary, belonging to the surface rather than to the core of his thought and teaching.

A Persecutor of Christians

Paul first appears in the New Testament in the role of a persecutor of the church: officiating at the martyrdom of Stephen, imprisoning Christians in Jerusalem, and bringing believers back who had fled for safety to areas outside of Palestine (Acts 7:58 - 8:3; 9:1, 2; I Cor. 15:9; Phil. 3:6). Some have argued that such action would hardly have been worthy a pupil of so tolerant a teacher as Gamaliel I, whose words in Acts 5:34-39 are certainly an example of moderation in the midst of frenzy. But what must be noticed is that in Pharisaic eyes, at least, the situation faced by Gamaliel and that which confronted the young rabbi Saul were quite different. Previous to Gamaliel's advice, it is recorded that the church's witness concerned the Lordship, Messiahship, and Saviorship of Jesus — His heaven-ordained death, His victorious resurrection, and His present status as exalted

Redeemer. The earliest Christians preached in terms mainly functional, without explicating the fullness of doctrine which lay in the substratum of their convictions. To the Sanhedrin, and especially to the Sadducean and priestly element instigating the early suppressions (Acts 4:1-22; 5:17-40), such teaching not only caused turmoil to orderly rule, but, more important, impinged upon their own authority. To the more noble and tolerant of the Pharisees, however, the Jerusalem Christians were yet within the scope of Judaism and not to be treated as heretics. The divine claims for Jesus the Christ were yet to be explicated unequivocally, and the Jewish believers gave no evidence of laxness in the observance of the Law because of their new beliefs. But between the time of Gamaliel's advice and Paul's action there appeared in the proclamation of the Christians what was to most Jews an ominous element of apostasy. In Acts 6 and 7, it is recorded that Stephen began to apply the doctrine of Jesus' Messiahship to the area of Jewish law. He probably was baited on this topic by returning Diaspora Jews who had moved to the homeland with a desire to keep the Law more rigidly, and who now were concerned about the Christians' attitude toward it. Undoubtedly Stephen had a real interest in the subject himself. But this was a dangerous path to tread. It was one which even the apostles were not ready to take, though it lay inherent in their commitment to Jesus as the Messiah. In Jewish eyes, Stephen's message was apostasy of the foulest kind; especially since it was voiced by one who had probably returned to the Holy City earlier motivated by religious ardor, but who was now most vociferous against all that he had formerly professed. Had Gamaliel faced this aspect of Christianity earlier, his attitude would surely have been different. With the whole basis of Judaism thus threatened, Paul's action could have been taken with the full approval of his honored teacher.

The rationale for such drastic action may be related to the prevalent view that while nothing could be done either to hurry or to frustrate entirely the coming of the Messianic Age, transgression and apostasy within the nation could delay it. Rabbi Simeon ben Yohai is credited with saying: "Like as when a man who brings together two ships, and binds them together with ropes and cords, and builds a palace upon them; while the ships are lashed together, the palace stands; when they drift apart it cannot stand" (Sifre Deut, Barakah 346; cf. also 1QS 9.20-21). And the Pharisaic endeavor to "build a hedge about the Law" by means of spelling out in detail the various biblical prescriptions was motivated in large part by the desire to keep Israel unified in its worship of God, especially during the times of "Messianic travail" in which many thought they were living. Zealous for the Law and eager to keep Israel united in days of approaching Messianic blessing, Paul early directed his efforts against Jewish believers in Jesus of Nazareth; for, as he saw it, their leader had been discredited by crucifixion and their schismatic preaching could only further delay Israel's promised Messianic Age.

Paul's action could also have been easily justified biblically. Numbers 25:1-5 speaks of Moses ordering the destruction of the immoral Israelites at Baal-peor, just prior to the people's entrance into Canaan. And Numbers 25:6-15 recounts the turning away of God's wrath by one man, Phinehas, who received God's praise for his zeal to put apostasy out of Israel — even to the killing of two of the chief offenders himself. To Paul, the situations then and in his day could have seemed analogous: Israel's near-entrance into the land with the near-Messianic kingdom, and the similar apostasies which could but further delay God's blessings. The activities of Mattathias and the Hasidim some two centuries earlier in rooting out apostasy among their own people (I Macc. 2:23-28, 42-48) may also have been his model; and the exhortation of II Maccabees 6:13 may even have rung in his ears: "For indeed it is a mark of great kindness when the impious are not let alone for a long time, but punished at once." With such precedents, coupled with the rising tide of Jewish Messianic expectancy, sufficient motivation was at hand for Paul to take upon himself the grisly task of uprooting what he believed to be apostasy. Much as one might recoil at the thought of so-called "righteous crusades" and "holy wars," he cannot deny that Judaism has many examples of such purgings, and that Judaism looked upon those undertaken at strategic moments in the nation's history as worthy of highest praise. But, though undoubtedly earnest and motivated by a desire to do God's will as he understood it, Paul was actually — as he later came to realize — opposing God "ignorantly in unbelief" (I Tim. 1:13).

The Tension of His Jewish Experience

It has frequently been suggested that Paul had an unhappy adolescence, crushed under the legalism and casuistry of his religion and longing for something of love and inwardness. This supposition is based in large measure on an autobiographical interpretation of Romans 7:7-25, wherein Paul is viewed as describing a time in his boyhood when he came to realize the awful demands of the Law and was therefore plunged into a perpetual and fruitless struggle with an uneasy conscience. It has sometimes also been supposed that this tension was the basis for his persecution of Christians: that he was attempting to externalize the conflict within by identifying what he detested in himself with some other body and was trying to silence his doubts by activity.

It is significant, however, that Paul's discussion of the relation of the Old Covenant and the New in Second Corinthians 3:7-18 does not present a contrast between a crushing legalism and a new prophetism. Rather, it is between what "once had splendor" and what is of "much more" and "surpassing splendor" (II Cor. 3:10, 11). It is true that he speaks of the Old Covenant as "the dispensation of death" (II Cor. 3:7) and "the dispensation of condemnation" (II Cor. 3:9). But he also insists that, though in relation to the surpassing splendor of the New Covenant the Law's glory is passing, it "came with splendor" (II Cor. 3:7, 11). In Galatians 4 he speaks of the Old Covenant as a bondage (vv. 1-7) and a slavery (vv. 21-31), but only in relation to the liberty found in Christ Jesus. Elsewhere, Paul talks as though his pre-Christian life had been entirely free from qualms of guilt and pangs of conscience, recalling for his converts his feeling of heady abandon in outstripping his fellow students in the rabbinic curriculum, his eager zeal for the traditions of his fathers, and his confidence of being blameless in the eyes of the Law (Gal. 1:14; Phil. 3:4-6; Acts 22:3; 26:4, 5).

Therefore, it seems that Paul's early religious experience must be interpreted along the lines of the normal Jewish response of his day: a rejoicing in the Law of God and a self-congratulation on his place in the divine favor (Rom. 2:17-20). He never speaks of his previous life in Judaism as one hideous mistake, nor as a bondage which anyone with an ounce of perception would have seen to have been in error. Rather, he continually measures it by the surpassing splendor and intimate communion found in Jesus Christ; and only on account of Christ was he prepared to call it, together with all human excellencies, something of the nature of rubbish (Phil 3:7-11). It was not dissatisfaction with the Law which prepared the way for Christ, but Christ who revealed to Paul the inadequacy of the Law and the ultimate futility of all human attainment.

What then was the tension which Paul experienced in Judaism, and which he found resolved in commitment to Christ? No doubt he had some appreciation of the inability of man to please God apart from divine mercy and strength, and probably he was repelled in some measure by the rising tide of externalism in his day. But these were matters shared with the better rabbis of the time, and not sufficient of themselves to effect any basic alteration in earlier commitments. The primary tension of Judaism, which dominates all the Old Testament and Jewish thought generally, is that of covenant promise and anticipated fulfillment. The religion of Israel is the religion of promise, with consummation reserved for the coming of the Messiah and the Messianic Age. And it was this tension, rather than any having to do with ethics, motivation or universalism, which Paul found resolved in commitment to Jesus of Nazareth as God's promised Messiah – the Messiah rejected, crucified, risen and now exalted.

3

Conversion and Early Ministry

Rome had recognized the high priests of Jerusalem as the titular rulers of their people, and in the alliances with the earlier Maccabean priest-kings, had included a reciprocal extradition clause (I Macc. 15:21-24). While the Sadducean priests no longer exercised the civil authority of their predecessors, evidently they retained the right of extradition in cases strictly religious. Thus, Paul, seeking the return of Jewish Christians (principally the Hellenistic Jewish believers), "went to the high priest and asked him for letters to the synagogues at Damascus, so that if he found any belonging to the Way, men or women, he might bring them bound to Jerusalem" (Acts 9:1,2; 22:5; 26:12).

The Circumstances of His Conversion

It was while traveling to Damascus to extradite Christians that Paul was confronted by the risen and glorified Christ in a manner which he considered comparable to the resurrection appearances to Peter, the other apostles and James (I Cor. 15:3-8). In Luke's account in Acts 9 and the apostle's speeches recorded in Acts 22 and 26, it is stated that at midday a light from heaven flashed about him and his cohorts, throwing them all to the ground and blinding Paul. Then a voice from heaven was heard to say, "Saul, Saul, why do you persecute me?" Paul asked regarding the identity of the speaker, and was told, "I am Jesus, whom you are persecuting." He was then instructed to rise and enter the city, and he would be told what to do. Stricken with blindness for three days, Paul was residing at the home of a man named Judas who lived on "the street called Straight," when a Christian disciple by the name of Ananias was sent by God to minister to him. It was through Ananias that Paul's sight was restored, he was baptized as a Christian, and further instructions were given him concerning God's purpose for his life.

A number of problems present themselves in comparing the accounts of Paul's conversion in Acts 9, 22, and 26; problems of the type frequently found in a comparison of the Synoptic Gospels – and, for that matter, found in any correlation of two or more separate narratives of any one historical event. The first concerns Luke's statement in Acts 9:7 that Paul's associates "stood speechless, *hearing the voice* but seeing no one," whereas Paul is represented in Acts 22:9 as saying that "those who were with me saw the light but *did not hear the voice* of the one who was speaking to me" and in Acts 26:14 as saying only "I heard a voice." This may be cited as a flagrant contradiction which the author of Acts unwittingly incorporated into his finished product; though probably it was understood by all concerned in the first century to mean only that while the whole group traveling to Damascus heard the sound of the voice from heaven, only Paul understood the articulated words.

A second problem concerns the reporting of the words heard by Paul. Whereas all three accounts have the words "Saul, Saul, why do you persecute me?" (Acts 9:4; 22:7; 26:14), if we accept the reading of the better ancient manuscripts only the third adds the phrase: "It hurts you to kick against the goads." The problem here, of course, has to do with the exact words of Jesus. Now it is well-known that "to kick against the goads" was a Greek idiom for opposition to deity (Euripides, *Bacchanals* 794-95; Aeschylus, *Prometheus* 324-25), and probably it was known within Jewish circles that this was something of a catch phrase or byword employed by the Gentiles. It is very well possible that in speaking to Agrippa II, Paul added this expression to the words of Jesus to make the king, whose native tongue and basic mentality were Greek, realize that correction by a voice from heaven meant rebuke from God Himself. It would hardly have been necessary for Paul (Acts 9) or for his Jewish audience at Jerusalem (Acts 22), since a voice from heaven *(bath kol)* had an unmistakable significance for any Jew. But in seeking to convey to a Gentile the revelation he had received – both in its explicit form and its implications – Paul seems to have found this Greek idiom a judicious vehicle for the expression of the full meaning of Jesus' words as he understood them.

The problem as to when Paul received his commission to preach to the Gentiles is somewhat more difficult to solve. Acts 9 indicates that it was through Ananias, who was sent to explicate the meaning of the Damascus road encounter. But Acts 22, though alluding to Ananias' ministry, associates the words "I will send you far away to the Gentiles" with a later vision while Paul was in the Jerusalem temple; and Acts 26 seems to imply that the commission came while he was on the Damascus road. For Paul, however, the meeting with Jesus, the ministry of Ananias, and the later vision of confirmation in the temple were probably all parts of the same event. In fact, when the details of that Gentile ministry were later spelled out more fully on his first missionary journey (see discussion below), he still viewed this as only an extension of that original charge. Probably, therefore, Acts 9 presents the actual sequence of events connected with Paul's conversion, Acts 22 adds the confirming vision at Jerusalem some three years later, and Acts 26 is an abbreviated testimony before the king – abbreviated so that the step by step account would not seem overly pedantic to his audience and since for Paul the events were inherently one.

The immediate sequel to his conversion was a three year period spent partly in Arabia (Nabatea?) and partly in Damascus (Gal. 1:17, 18). During this time Paul seems to have been re-evaluating his life and the Scriptures from a Christocentric perspective and witnessing to Jews that Jesus is "the Son of God" and "the Messiah" (Acts 9:20-22). Nothing is told about the importance of this period for Paul personally, though undoubtedly it was a time when many of the implications of his commitment to Jesus as God's promised Messiah and his commission to carry this message to the Gentiles were being spelled out under the guidance of the Spirit.

Conditioning Antecedents

There is no evidence in the New Testament relative to whether Paul had ever seen Jesus during His earthly ministry or not – the statement of Second Corinthians 5:16 about having known Christ after the flesh is correctly interpreted by the RSV to mean that his former estimate of Jesus had been based on worldly standards alone, and thus has no bearing on the question at hand. Certainly, however, he had a vivid impression of Jesus' character and claims during these early days, as gathered from Jewish reports and Christian witnesses and as seen through Pharisaic eyes. No man carries on a campaign of persecution without having what he believes to be sufficient information to fan his hatred. Paul's knowledge of Jesus prior to his conversion seems only to have inflamed his antagonism, being convinced as he was that Jesus was a discredited impostor and His followers actually dangerous to the nation's future in preaching their delusions.

Many have suggested that Paul's conversion was prepared for by his contacts with Christians, and that unconsciously he was being conditioned by the logic of their arguments, the dynamic quality of their lives, and their fortitude under oppression. Certainly Luke makes the historical connection between the martyrdom of Stephen, the persecution of believers, and the conversion of Paul. But the suggestion that a logical connection is involved is nowhere certain. It is, of course, impossible to speak with any certainty about what was going on in Paul's subconscious mind, for psychoanalysis two millennia or so later is hardly a fruitful exercise. Yet it is probable that Paul had taken up his task of persecution with full knowledge of the earnestness of his opponents, the stamina of the martyr, and the agony he would necessarily inflict. Fanaticism was not so foreign to the Palestine of his day as to leave him unaware of these facts, and it is quite possible that he was prepared for the emotional strain involved in persecuting those he believed to be misguided and dangerous foes. Nor need we suppose that the logic of the Christian preachers greatly affected him. His later references to the scandal of the cross indicate that for him this was the great stumbling block, which no amount of logic or verbal gymnastics could remove (I Cor. 1:23; Gal. 5:11; cf. Justin's *Dialogue with Trypho* 32, 89).

While his life in Judaism and his contacts with Christians were later acknowledged to have confirmatory value, they seem not to have been factors which drove Paul inevitably to a point of crisis. Only the Damascus encounter with Christ was powerful enough to cause the young Jewish rabbi to reconsider the death of Jesus; only his meeting with the risen Christ was sufficient to demonstrate that God had vindicated the claims and work of the

One he was opposing. Humanly speaking, Paul was immune to the Gospel. Although he was ready to follow evidence to its conclusion, he was sure that no evidence could overturn the verdict of the cross; that is, that Christ died the death of a criminal. But God gives sufficient evidence to the earnest to convince and lead them on. And therefore the eternal God "was pleased," as Paul says by way of reminiscence, "to reveal his Son to me" (Gal. 1:16). Thus Paul was arrested by Christ, and made His own (Phil. 3:12).

Resultant Convictions

Having been met by Christ on the way to Damascus, three convictions became inescapably obvious to Paul. In the first place, despite zeal, superior credentials, and an assurance of doing God's will (Rom. 9:4, 5; 10:2-4), his life and activities in Judaism lay under the rebuke of God. A voice from heaven had corrected him, and there was nothing more that could be said. He had held tenaciously to the Mosaic law as having *intrinsic* authority, but failed to appreciate that it also bore *instrumental* authority; that is, that it had been given as a custodian to lead men on to faith in Jesus Christ (Gal. 3:19-24). But now that Christ had come and the Gospel message had gone out, to refuse Him of whom the Law speaks and to venerate the letter above the Person who is its object, is to revert to "weak and beggarly elemental principles" (Gal. 3:25 - 4:11).

Secondly, he could not escape the conclusion that the Jesus whom he was persecuting was alive, exalted, and in some manner to be associated with God, the Father, whom Israel worshiped. He had therefore to revise his whole estimate of the life, teaching and death of the Nazarene, for God had obviously vindicated Him in a manner beyond dispute. Thus he was compelled to agree with the Christians that Christ's death on the cross, rather than discrediting Him as an impostor, was really God's provision for man's sin and was in fulfillment of prophecy. And he was compelled to acknowledge that Christ's resurrection, also in fulfillment of prophecy, was proof of these facts and provides life to those who will receive Him (I Cor. 15:3ff). In commitment to this risen Lord, he found (1) the ancient tension of covenant promise and anticipated fulfillment brought to consummation, and (2) true righteousness and intimate fellowship with God.

A third conviction which was unmistakably clear to Paul was that he had been appointed by Jesus Christ to be an apostle to the Gentiles, delivering to them the message of a crucified and risen Lord and bringing them into the unity of one body in Christ (Rom. 11:13; 15:16; Gal. 1:11-16; Eph. 3:8). There is no consciousness in Paul that he differed from the earlier apostles on the matter of the content of the Gospel. But there is the settled conviction reflected in his writings that he had been given a new understanding of the pattern of redemptive history. This he refers to as "my gospel" (Rom. 2:16; 16:25), always asserting that it came to him via a revelation given by Jesus Christ (Gal. 1: 1, 11, 12; Eph. 3:2, 3). Although in further visions and providential circumstances he was to understand more clearly that the Gospel involves full equality of Jew and Gentile before God and the legitimacy of a direct approach to the Gentile world in the Christian mission, it was his constant habit to relate his Gentile commission firmly and directly to his conversion.

Ministry to Diaspora Jews

The three years following Paul's conversion were spent in and around Damascus (Acts 9:19-22; Gal. 1:17, 18), the biblical "Arabia" probably having reference to the area ruled by the Nabateans and of which Damascus was at various times the principal city. During this time Paul proclaimed the Sonship and Messiahship of Jesus (Acts 9:20, 22), and at the end of his residence in Damascus he was forced to leave by means of a basket let down over the city wall (Acts 9:23-25; II Cor. 11:32, 33). His reference to this incident in Second Corinthians indicates that it happened at a time when Damascus was ruled by the Nabatean king Aretas. Now Damascene coinage proves that the city was under the direct rule of Rome in A.D. 33-34. This means that Paul's departure from the city, occurring as it did during the supremacy of Aretas, probably took place in the final years of the emperor Tiberius, though possibly after the accession of Caligula in A.D. 37. On this basis, Paul's conversion may be dated somewhere between A.D. 32 and 35; though precision is manifestly impossible apart from further data.

Arriving in Jerusalem, Paul took up the ministry to Hellenistic Jews – a ministry that had been neglected since Stephen's death. But he faced the same opposition which he himself once had led, and seems to have gotten into the same difficulty as that which cost Stephen his life (Acts 9:26-29). This was in all likelihood the visit of fifteen days of which he speaks in Galatians 1:18-20. Evidently the Jerusalem church did not care to go through another series of events such as followed Stephen's preaching, for when they realized what was taking place "they brought him down to Caesarea, and sent him off to Tarsus" (Acts 9:30). Though it might seem to have been something of a personal rebuff from Paul's perspective, such a departure was under divine approval, for in the temple he received a vision which not only confirmed his apostleship to the Gentiles, but warned him to flee Jerusalem (Acts 22:17-21).

Paul is not mentioned in the period between these experiences in Jerusalem and his ministry at Antioch (Acts 11:25-30), though from his words in Galatians 1:21-24 it seems fairly certain that he continued his witness to dispersed Jews in Caesarea and his hometown of Tarsus. The cordiality of the Christians at Caesarea at the end of his third missionary journey lends some credence to an earlier association with Philip and the believers there. Many of the hardships and trials enumerated in Second Corinthians 11:23-27 may stem from situations faced at Caesarea and Tarsus during those days, for they find no place in the records of the later missionary journeys in Acts. Perhaps the ecstatic experience of Second Corinthians 12:1-4 also comes from this period in his life.

Ministry to God-fearing Gentiles

In the expansion of the church occasioned by the persecutions in Jerusalem, certain believers who originally came from Cyprus and Cyrene carried the Gospel to Antioch in Syria and included Greeks in the scope of their ministry (Acts 11:19-21). There is some textual uncertainty as to whether the "great number" who heard their message and believed is to be understood as Greeks in the sense of Gentiles or Greeks in the sense of Hellenistic Jews, as in Acts 6:1. But in that the evidence from the manuscripts slightly favors the former and they are distinguished from Jews in the passage itself, it seems best to conclude that these Christian missionaries carried on a witness to Gentiles as an adjunct to their ministry to Jews – that is, through the synagogues and to God-fearing Gentiles ("Proselytes of the Gate"). When news of this ministry to both Jews and God-fearing Gentiles reached Jerusalem, the church there sent Barnabas, a Levite originally from Cyprus (Acts 4:36), to check on conditions at Antioch. We read that "when he came and saw the grace of God, he was glad, and he exhorted them all to remain faithful to the Lord with steadfast purpose; for he was a good man, full of the Holy Spirit and of faith" (Acts 11:22-24).

It was Barnabas who brought Paul to Antioch, having gone to Tarsus to find him (Acts 11:25, 26). Barnabas had earlier acted on Paul's behalf when there was suspicion about his conversion among the Jerusalem disciples (Acts 9:27). And now, knowing of his commission to the Gentiles, remembering the impact of his testimony, conscious of his abilities, and needing help in the ministry among the Gentile converts, Barnabas involved Paul in the work at Antioch. Here Paul joined not only Barnabas, but also Symeon "who was called Niger" (a black man), Lucius of Cyrene, and Manaen who had been raised in Herod's court (Acts 13:1). The Greek construction of the passage suggests that Barnabas, Symeon and Lucius functioned as "prophets," which probably means that they were the ones principally engaged in the task of proclaiming the good news of salvation in Christ Jesus. Manaen and Paul were the "teachers," which seems to signify that theirs was the primary responsibility of instructing the converts concerning biblical foundations and implications. In this capacity Paul ministered for a year.

In such an enterprise, Paul was, of course, involved in a mission to Gentiles. And he may have thought this to be all that was involved in the commission received at his conversion. It is probable, however, that the Antioch mission in those early days was carried out exclusively in terms of the synagogue and as an adjunct to the ministry to Jews, without any consideration being given to whether it were proper to appeal more widely and directly to Gentiles. Believers in Jesus at Antioch were probably related in some way to the synagogue; whether they were Jewish or Gentile in background. And thus in the eyes of many Jewish believers, the conversion of God-fearing Gentiles who had come under the ministry of Judaism to some extent prior to their allegiance to Jesus would have been viewed as somewhat similar to that of Jewish proselytes. However, others within the city, evidently non-believers with more perception regarding the Antioch church's essential commitments and in anticipation of the later debates as to whether believers in Jesus had an identity of their own or belonged to the Jewish commonwealth, called them "Christians" – that is, "Christ followers" or "those of the household of Christ."

During Paul's ministry in Antioch, a Jerusalemite prophet by the name of Agabus prophesied of an approaching famine, and the church at Antioch sent aid to their brethren in the Holy City by the hands of Barnabas and Paul (Acts 11:17-30). The famine is spoken of in Acts as occurring during the time of Claudius (A.D. 41-54). It can, however, be dated more precisely at about A.D. 46, by (1) information from the Roman historians Tacitus and Suetonius concerning a widespread famine about this time, (2) evidence preserved in the papyri concerning the high price of grain in Egypt also about this time, and (3) Josephus' account of the Egyptian queen Helena. A convert to Judaism, Helena gathered supplies from Egypt and Cyprus for famine-stricken Jerusalem soon after her arrival on a pilgrimage to the city about A.D. 45 or 46 (Antiquities XX.51-53).

The understanding of Paul's activity at this time is heavily dependent upon the answer to the ancient conundrum of the relation of the two Jerusalem visits mentioned in Galatians to the three early Jerusalem visits reported in Acts. While most accept the first visit of Galatians 1:18-20 to be that of Acts 9:26-29 (as presented above), many feel that Galatians 2:1-10 is really to be identified with the Jerusalem Council of Acts 15. The issues are complex and have far-reaching consequences. The simplest solution which results in the most satisfactory and convincing reconstruction and leaves the fewest loose ends, however, is that Galatians 2:1-10 corresponds to the "famine visit" of Acts 11:30. On this view, the temporal adverb "then" of Galatians 2:1 has the same antecedent as that of Galatians 1:18 – both referring back to Paul's conversion. His conversion would then have occurred (allowing some flexibility in rounding off the years) about A.D. 33; his escape from Damascus and subsequent visit to Jerusalem, about A.D. 36; and his "famine visit" to Jerusalem some fourteen years after his conversion, about A.D. 46. And on this view, the reference to having gone to Jerusalem "by revelation" in Galatians 2:2 and Agabus' prophecy of Acts 11:28 could be related.

If the equation of Galatians 2:1-10 and Acts 11:30 is correct, Paul and Barnabas, having been sent by the Antioch church with aid for stricken believers of Jerusalem, then took the opportunity to hold a private discussion with James, Peter and John on the issues of the nature of the Gospel, the validity of a mission to Gentiles, and the relation of Gentile converts to the Law. They also took along Titus, an uncircumcised Gentile Christian, whose presence might have been intended as something of a test case. He may, however, have been included with no thought other than the help he would be on the mission – and, perhaps, with some failure to appreciate fully the pressures that could be brought to bear because of him. Paul mentions the reactions of two groups at Jerusalem in his report of the conversations: (1) that of certain "false brethren secretly brought in, who slipped in to spy out our freedom which we have in Christ Jesus, that they might bring us into bondage" (Gal. 2:4, 5); and (2) that of the "pillar" apostles in the Jerusalem church (Gal. 2:6-10). Whether the pseudo-brethren were Jewish spies sent to see what treachery the Christians were planning with Gentiles or whether they were angry Jewish Christian disputants who threatened to publish what was happening at Antioch unless Titus were circumcised, we cannot say. But the extremely important point to note is that, despite mounting pressures and possibly some uncertainties, the Jerusalem apostles agreed with Paul on the substance of the Gospel and the validity of a mission to Gentiles, though, admittedly, they felt themselves committed to a different sphere of ministry than his. Moreover, they made no demands as to the necessity of Gentile believers being circumcised. As yet, however, the issue of a direct approach to Gentiles apart from the ministrations of the synagogue did not come to the fore. That was to be raised on the first missionary journey, and would be the occasion for resurrecting the whole complex of issues again at the Jerusalem Council.

4

First Missionary Journey

The first missionary journey of Paul (Acts 13 - 14) is often treated as something of a "filler" inserted by Luke as a transition to get from the circumstances of the Jerusalem church under Herod Agrippa I (Acts 12) to the Jerusalem Council (Acts 15), or relegated to the status of a displaced aspect of the Pauline missionary endeavors which presumably occurred much later. But to class this period of Paul's labors as insignificant, invented or misplaced, overlooks an important advance in the preaching of the Gospel and destroys any adequate rationale for events which follow.

The Course of the Mission

While Paul and Barnabas were ministering at Antioch in Syria, the Holy Spirit directed that they be released from their duties in the church there and sent out to minister more widely (Acts 13:2, 3). The means by which the Spirit so directed them are not expressly given, though there are some hints that it was through the convergence of three factors: (1) an urging within the apostles themselves, for they were fasting at the time they received the explicit direction; (2) a prophetic utterance on the part of one of the members of the church, similar perhaps to Agabus' word earlier; and (3) the assurance to the body of believers that this was indeed the will of God, which was given after fasting and prayer. The subject ("they") of Acts 13:3 is somewhat difficult to determine grammatically, and may refer to the "prophets and teachers" of verse one. On this reading, it was the other three leaders in the Antioch church who, after fasting and prayer, "laid their hands on them and sent them off." On analogy with Acts 15:2, however, where there appears the same linguistic phenomenon of a pronominal suffix lacking an expressed antecedent and where the subject is later identified as "the church" (Acts 15:3), it is probable that the body of believers as a whole was involved in determining the will of the Lord, laying hands on the apostles and sending them out. "So," Acts 13:4 concludes, they were "sent out by the Holy Spirit." They took with them John Mark, a young man from Jerusalem (Acts 12:12) and the cousin of Barnabas (Col. 4:10).

Leaving Antioch and its port city Seleucia, the missionary party set out for Barnabas' native Cyprus. And from Salamis on the east to Paphos on the west, they preached the Gospel throughout the island, though, always "in the synagogues of the Jews" (Acts 13:5). At Paphos, however, the proconsul Sergius Paulus requested that they present their message before him. The meeting may have been intended only as an inquisition into the nature of their preaching so that the proconsul might be in a position to head off any features which could cause disturbance within the Jewish community on the island. As a "command performance" of a somewhat devious type, it could hardly have been avoided. But despite the opposition of Bar-Jesus the magician, and impressed by the effect of the curse pronounced by Paul upon this "son of the devil," Sergius Paulus believed (Acts 13:6-12). Here was something quite unexpected, for the Roman proconsul seems not to have been related in any way to Judaism or its institutions. Here was a situation which could hardly have appeared otherwise to the apostles than the counterpart of the conversion of the Roman centurion Cornelius (Acts 10:1 - 11:18); indeed, in some ways going beyond the case of Cornelius. But though the Jerusalem church seems never to have taken Cornelius' conversion as establishing a precedent for its ministry, for its mission was to Israel, Paul, whose call was to the Gentiles, undoubtedly saw in this incident at Paphos something more of what a mission to Gentiles logically involved. At this point in the record, significantly, he begins to be called by his Roman name, Paul, rather than his Jewish name, Saul (Acts 13:9); for from this point on he is prepared to meet a Gentile of the empire as himself a member of that empire, apart from any necessary common ground as supplied by the synagogue. And from this time on, with but two understandable exceptions (Acts 14:12; 15:12), Paul's name always appears first in connection with that of Barnabas.

From Cyprus the missioners sailed to Perga in Pamphylia, on the mainland of Asia Minor (Acts 13:13). No account of a ministry in Perga at this time is given, though on their return visit they preached there (Acts 14:25). The usual explanation for this bypassing of Perga and moving on to Antioch of Pisidia is that Paul was probably ill, perhaps with a case of malaria, and thus he redirected his mission to gain the higher ground of the plateau to the north. While this may be true, it can as readily be postulated that the ignoring of Perga at this time was largely because of uncertainty within the missionary party itself regarding the validity of a direct approach to Gentiles. Undoubtedly after Paphos the discussion among the missionaries concerning their further ministry centered on the implications of Sergius Paulus' conversion.

It was at this time, the account in Acts tells us, that John Mark left the group and returned to Jerusalem. Perhaps it was this reconsideration of their mission, and the inferences being drawn by Paul from recent events, that were the real reasons for Mark's departure. While Paul saw in the Paphos experience the explication of his original commission, John Mark may very well have felt concerned for the effect such news of a direct Christian ministry to Gentiles would have in Jerusalem and upon the Jerusalem church – and wanted no part in it himself. Explanations of Mark's defection which stress homesickness, the rigors of travel, a change in leadership within the group, or an illness of Paul necessitating a changed itinerary are at best only partial, and at worst unconvincing. They fail to account for the obstinate opposition of Paul toward Mark as recorded in Acts 15:37-39, which implies that Mark's departure was for more than merely personal reasons.

At Antioch of Pisidia, Paul proclaimed to Jews and "devout converts to Judaism" assembled in the synagogue on the sabbath day that Jesus is the Messiah and Savior promised in Holy Writ (Acts 13:14-43). On the next sabbath, however, when a great number of Gentiles expressed their interest in Paul's message, the Jewish community went on record as being in opposition to the Gospel; and Paul turned directly to the Gentiles in continuation of his mission in the city, finding great receptivity among them (Acts 13:44-49). Here the typical pattern of the Pauline mission was established: an initial proclamation to Jews and Gentile adherents to Judaism, whether full proselytes or more loosely associated, and then, being refused further audience in the synagogue, a direct ministry among Gentiles. This pattern was followed in every city with a Jewish population visited by Paul. We know this from Acts, with the exception of Athens.

Also at Pisidian Antioch the pattern of opposition to Paul was established (Acts 13:50). The Jews found occasion to reject his message on the grounds that he was willing to approach Gentiles apart from the institutions of the ancestral faith. As Paul saw it, Jewish obstinancy made such action necessary if Gentiles were to hear the Gospel and be brought to the one true God. But as they viewed it, this disproved the claim that in Jesus of Nazareth the promises to the fathers have been brought to fulfillment. For the Jewish leaders, Christianity was a religion to be sharply distinguished from Judaism and its Scriptures – as Paul's willingness to work apart from its institutions demonstrated – and therefore was not entitled to protection under the Roman law of one religion for one people. While Christianity sought legitimacy in the eyes of Rome by nestling under the wings of Judaism, its mode of approach proved that it was really an invasion requiring active repulsion. Thus the Jews worked through "the devout women of high standing" (proselyte wives of Roman officials?), who influenced their husbands to declare Paul and his party disruptive to the "Peace of Rome." On such a pretext persecution arose in Antioch, and the missionary party was expelled. And that pattern was often reproduced throughout the Pauline missionary journeys.

The ministry at Iconium resulted in "a great company, both of Jews and of Greeks," coming to Christ (Acts 14:1). Again, however, the issue was raised concerning Christianity's claim to continuity with the religion of Israel and to protection as a legal religion; and when the local authorities sided with the Jewish view and persecution became intolerable, the apostles fled to Lystra and Derbe (Acts 14:2-6). The reference to Lystra and Derbe as "cities of Lycaonia" (Acts 14:6) suggests that Iconium was a city of another district. Because of the location of these three cities in the same geographic area, this has been cited in the past as an example of Luke's inaccuracy of details. The research of William M. Ramsay, however, has shown that in the period between A.D. 37 and 72 – and only during this period – Lystra and Derbe were ruled directly by the Romans whereas Iconium was governed by Antiochus; and that while the region in which Lystra and Derbe were located was officially known as Galatica Lycaonia and that of Iconium as Lycaonia Antiochiana, more popularly they were called Lycaonia and Phrygia. The fact that Lystra and Derbe were cities under a different jurisdiction than Iconium was therefore a matter of real importance to Paul and Barnabas, for in crossing the regional border they were able to elude the Phrygian authorities.

Lystra and Derbe proved to be fruitful areas for the sowing of the Gospel (Acts 14:21), though not without their difficulties. One convert at Lystra on this first journey was Timothy (Acts 16:1; 20:4), whom Paul later included as a member of his missionary team. A disappointment at Lystra was the fickleness of the people in their response to the power of God and the issues involved in Paul's preaching. On the one hand, having witnessed the cripple healed at the command of Paul, they were ready to worship the apostles as the gods Zeus (the Roman god Jupiter) and Hermes (the Roman god Mercury) come in the guise of men. Then the apostles were hard-pressed to quiet the mob, speaking impassionately in an attempt to redirect their adoration (Acts 14:8-18). Yet, on the other hand, they seem to have been easily persuaded that if these men were not gods, they were probably impostors; and under the urging of Jews from Antioch and Iconium, their veneration turned to hatred and the actual stoning of Paul (Acts 14:19).

The initial and wildly emotional response of the people is understandable to some extent in light of an ancient legend which the poet Ovid retells, and which was probably familiar to many in the region of southern Asia Minor. According to the legend *(Metamorphoses* VIII), Zeus and Hermes once came to the area disguised as mortals seeking lodging. But though they asked at a thousand homes, they were not accepted into any. Finally, asking at a humble and small home built only of straw and reeds, they were received by an elderly couple, Philemon and his wife Baucis, who provided them with a banquet which strained their poor resources, but which was offered willingly.

In appreciation, the gods transformed their cottage into a temple with a golden roof and marble columns. They also appointed Philemon and Baucis to be the priest and priestess of the temple; and instead of eventually dying, they were transformed into an oak tree and a linden. However, in vengeance on the people who showed no hospitality, the gods destroyed their houses. Just where this was supposed to have taken place is vague, Ovid saying only that it occurred in "the Phrygian hill-country." Nonetheless, it appears that, remembering the legend and seeing the healing of the man lame from birth, the people of Lystra believed that the gods Zeus and Hermes had returned. They wanted to pay the proper homage rather than suffer the consequences.

The first missionary journey probably took place during the years A.D. 46 through 48; though, admittedly, this is only an estimate based on the dating of earlier and later events. Having spent about two years evangelizing Cyprus and southern Asia Minor, the apostles revisited the churches which they had planted – instructing the believers further in the doctrine of Christ, exhorting them to remain faithful to the Lord despite opposition, and appointing elders for the continuance of the ministry (Acts 14:21-23). Then after preaching in Perga, they returned to Antioch in Syria. And having gathered the believers at Antioch together, "they declared all that God had done with them, and *how he had opened a door of faith to the Gentiles*" (Acts 14:27).

The Significance of the Mission

That Gentiles are to be included in the blessings of Israel is a recurring theme in the Old Testament (e.g., Gen. 22:18; 26:4; 28:14; Isa. 49:6; 55:5, 6; Zeph. 3:9, 10; Zech. 8:22). It was the underlying presupposition in all Jewish proselytizing (Matt. 23:15; Pirke Aboth 1:12), and it was implicit in the sermons of Peter at Pentecost and in the house of Cornelius (Acts 2:39; 10:35). That Gentiles were already accepted as Christians by the church is evidenced in the cases of Cornelius and the God-fearing Gentiles of Syrian Antioch. But the correlative conviction of the whole of Judaism was that Israel alone was God's appointed agent for the administration of these blessings. It was through the nation and the ministrations of its institutions that the Gentiles would have a part in God's redemptive program and share in His favor. And there seems to have been no expectation on the part of the earliest Jewish Christians that this procedure would be materially altered; though in these "last days," of course, it was through the church as the true Israel and faithful remnant within the nation that God was working.

In the experience of the church, Gentiles had always (with only one exception) come to acknowledge Jesus as the Messiah and their Lord after having sustained some relation to Judaism, either as proselytes (Nicolaus of Acts 6:5, and possibly the eunuch of Acts 8:26-39) or as "Proselytes of the Gate" (the "Greeks" of Acts 11:20-26). Only Cornelius' conversion did not conform to this pattern, but that was viewed as quite exceptional and not as the occasion for a revision of policy – though it was later cited in support of Paul's procedure (Acts 15:7-11). Though Paul had earlier discussed with the leaders of the Jerusalem church the commission which he had received to minister to Gentiles, evidently at the time both he and they had in mind an outreach that would be conducted through the synagogues exclusively.

The practice inaugurated by Paul on his first missionary journey, however, went far beyond these expectations. The conversion of Sergius Paulus apart from any previous connection with the synagogue had become for Paul that which the conversion of Cornelius had not become for the Jerusalem apostles, for in it he saw God providentially explicating more fully what was involved in a mission to Gentiles. Furthermore, God had wonderfully stamped His approval on such a methodology by the increasing number of Gentiles whose hearts He had touched. While the synagogue was the appropriate place to begin his ministry in each city, offering as it did an audience of both Jews and Gentiles that had every reason to be spiritually sensitive and theologically alert, it was not the only sphere wherein his ministry could be carried out. Jew and Gentile stood on an equal footing before God (Rom. 2:1 - 3:20), and with differing backgrounds and sensibilities, they could be appealed to separately and in a different manner.

This was Paul's "gospel," of which he speaks in Galatians 1:11 - 2:10. It was not a difference in content, but a distinction in the pattern of redemptive logistics. By revelation, the nature of his ministry had been indicated; by circumstances providentially controlled, specifics of that call had been explicated. Jew and Gentile stood as equals before God in condemnation, in spiritual need, and in their status before God when they were renewed "in Christ." As Paul wrote in later life, "the mystery was made known to me by revelation . . . which was not made known to the sons of men in other generations as it has now been revealed to his holy apostles and prophets by the Spirit; that is, how the Gentiles are fellow heirs, members of the same body, and partakers of the promise in Christ Jesus through the gospel" (Eph. 3:3-6).

Jewish Responses to the Mission

In turning to the question of Jewish responses to Paul's first missionary journey, one is immediately confronted by the thorny issue of the relation of the Galatian letter to the periods of Paul's ministry; for if it relates to the period under discussion, it furnishes extremely important evidence for the subject at hand. Much has been written as to whether in the letter Paul was using "Galatia" in an ethnological sense addressing people of Celtic descent (Gauls) in the north of the Roman province of Galatia, and therefore writing on his third missionary journey, or employing the term in a political sense addressing a mixed population living in the southern portion of the province, and thus possibly writing after his first missionary journey or early on his second. Every work on "special introduction" treats the literary and historical matters that pertain to this question, and there is no need to reproduce them here. One point drawn from the Pauline polemic in Galatians, however, needs to be made at this time: that Paul's silence in Galatians regarding the decision of the Jerusalem Council forces the irreconcilable dilemma of declaring that either (1) the Acts account of the Council and its decision in Acts 15 is pure fabrication, or (2) the letter to the Galatians was written prior to the Council.

The fact that Paul felt obliged to give an explanation of his visits to Jerusalem implies that his adversaries in Galatia had been using one or both of those visits in some manner detrimental to his position and authority. And that Paul should take up a discussion of his contacts with the Jerusalem leaders, and for one reason or another fail to mention the decision reached at the Council (accepting for the moment both the veracity of Acts 15 and a late date for the composition of Galatians), is entirely inconceivable. The decision of the Council was the *coup de grâce* to the whole conflict. Nor will it do to argue that since the decrees promulgated at the end of the Council could have been set forth apart from Paul's knowledge (which is highly improbable), there is also the possibility that Paul was unaware of the major decision of the Council. Whatever is said of the decrees themselves, the overriding decision of the Council was so completely in harmony with Paul's view that there is no reason for him being uninformed or that it be kept from him. Either Paul did not know of such a decision when he wrote to the Galatians because that decision as recorded in Acts 15 has no basis in fact, or he did not know of it because he wrote to the Galatians before it had been reached. And while it is often asserted otherwise, one need not conclude that the only recourse is to skepticism of the account in Acts.

Similarly, on the assumption that the Antioch episode reported in Galatians 2:11-21 took place after the Jerusalem Council, Paul's recounting of the clash between himself and Peter at the appearance of "certain men from James" undercuts his whole argument and turns to the advantage of the Judaizing opponents, and not to himself – for it would bring to light his recognition of a cleavage between himself and the Jerusalem leaders that was only superficially patched up at the Council. The inclusion of such an incident at a time before the Council is understandable. But to use it in support of his argument after the Council leaves some doubt regarding the logical ability of the apostle. Rather than attempt to save Paul's rationality by reversing the order of events in Galatians, thus making Galatians 2:11-21 refer to a time before the Council and Galatians 2:1-10 apply to the Council, as some have suggested, we should accept the most natural interpretation: that all of these biographical statements were written prior to the Council. Admittedly, there are difficulties of detail with an early dating of the letter, but the problems confronted in accepting the later date are damaging to any high view of the rationality of Paul or the veracity of Acts.

Accepting, then, the theory that Galatians was written to converts living in the southern part of the Roman province of Galatia and at a time prior to the Jerusalem Council, the letter is Paul's earliest extant writing, being composed probably about A.D. 49 at Antioch in Syria – or perhaps on the journey from Antioch to Jerusalem. Important for consideration here, therefore, is the fact that the letter to the Galatians seems to reflect the responses toward Paul and his Gentile mission of three types of Jews: (1) the unbelieving Jews of Jerusalem, (2) the apostolic leaders in the Jerusalem church, and (3) the Judaizers.

The interpretation of the Antioch episode (Gal. 2:11-21) depends largely on the identification of "those of the circumcision" (as it may be literally translated) of verse twelve, who were feared. Usually the phrase is rendered as "the circumcision party" (RSV, Moffatt), and understood to mean legalistic and rigorous Jewish believers who came to Antioch "from James." On this basis, the characters in the drama are frequently drawn up as follows: (1) James and his emissaries, representing the Judaizing element within the Jerusalem church; (2) Peter, the Jewish Christians of Antioch, and Barnabas, who were not legalists as the first group but who would bow to the authority of Jerusalem Christianity as represented by James; (3) Paul as the sole champion of Gentile freedom and equality; and (4) the Gentile converts in Antioch who stood in the background looking on. But while Luke uses this phrase in Acts 10:45 and 11:2 for Jewish Christians, it is never so employed by Paul. In the apostle's writings, "those of the circumcision" and "the circumcised" when employed in an abstract sense always refer to Jews in general (Rom. 3:30; 4:9; 4:12; 15:8; Gal. 2:7-9; Eph. 2:11; Col. 3:11; 4:11; the use in Titus 1:10 is indeterminate). Therefore, consistent with his use of "the circumcised" in the verses immediately preceding (Gal. 2:7-9), Galatians 2:12b should read, as J. B. Phillips correctly has it: Peter "withdrew and ate separately from the Gentiles – out of sheer fear of what *the Jews* might think." From such a statement we gather that the unbelieving Jews of Jerusalem were antagonistic to and repelled by Paul's endeavors, as the majority of their brethren in the Diaspora also proved to be.

In view of the Jewish reaction at home, the Christian apostles of Jerusalem were faced with the practical necessity of minimizing unnecessary conflicts that might arise between Judaism and the Christian mission. Therefore one should probably view the messengers "from James" as bringing, not an ultimatum from a faction of extremists, but an urgent warning that increasing rumors of Jewish Christian fraternizing with uncircumcised Gentiles in Antioch and southern Asia Minor were putting all the churches in Judea in considerable danger. In such a situation, Peter might have thought it expedient to modify his practice for a while until the danger abated; and the Antioch Jewish Christians, together with "even Barnabas" (Gal. 2:13), seem to have agreed with him. Paul, it must be noticed, did not accuse Peter of having wrong principles, but of being untrue to the principles he professed (Gal. 2:14ff). This suggests that in Paul's view Peter's action was undertaken for reasons of expediency, and not as a matter of principle as the Judaizers advocated. But though Peter's action was professedly only a matter of expediency, Paul saw that it did touch upon an essential principle. For to distinguish between Jewish and Gentile believers on this basis, even though temporarily and under external pressure, was to question ultimately the validity of those Gentiles' Christian faith, and to drive a wedge between the Jewish and the Gentile missions which could never be completely extricated.

Considerations of expediency, however, gave way in certain quarters to conclusions justified on principle. And as so often happens with the increase of pressure, emotional responses and pragmatically sanctioned procedures tended by some to become buttressed theologically. Thus certain Jewish Christians followed the Pauline circuit in southern Galatia preaching that it was theologically necessary for Gentile converts to become circumcised and devotees of the Mosaic law, and others from Jerusalem came to Antioch of Syria insisting that "unless you are circumcised according to the custom of Moses, you cannot be saved" (Acts 15:1). That behind these Judaizers stood James and Peter is a fiction which finds no support in historical fact; for while the Jerusalem apostles were vitally interested in reducing tensions between Judaism and Jewish Christianity wherever possible, they were not prepared to sacrifice the principles of the Gospel for the sake of expediency when they became aware of the implications involved. The Judaizers, on the other hand, while probably first justifying their legalism on grounds of expediency, were now also arguing on principle the necessity of circumcision and the keeping of the Law. According to First Thessalonians 2:14-16, Paul regarded unbelieving Jews as the ultimate source of opposition to the Gentile mission. Thus when he says in Galatians 6:13 that the Judaizers "desire to have you circumcised that they may glory in your flesh," he probably means it was so that they could point out to non-Christian Jews that the Gospel does in fact relate Gentiles to the Jewish world in some fashion. Undoubtedly the Judaizers thought of themselves as acting conscientiously. But as Paul viewed it, they wanted "a good showing in the flesh . . . only in order that they may not be persecuted for the cross of Christ" (Gal. 6:12).

5

The Jerusalem Council

The practice inaugurated by Paul on his first missionary journey of appealing directly to Gentiles was a matter of far-reaching concern at Jerusalem. In the Gentile churches, as well, issues needed to be clarified, especially in light of the claims and activities of the Judaizers. It was at the Council of Jerusalem, probably convened in the year A.D. 49, that matters came to a head and decisions were made which were to affect greatly the course of both the Christian mission to the Jews and that of Paul to the Gentiles.

The Issues Involved

As the true Israel and faithful remnant within the nation, the Jerusalem church naturally expected the Christian mission to proceed along lines laid out of old by God. Its *raison d'être* was built on this assumption. And in its pragmatic polemic, it could point to the fact that, with very few exceptions, commitment to Jesus did not make Jews less Jewish. In some cases, as a matter of fact, it even brought Gentiles who had been loosely associated with the synagogue into greater conformity to Jewish ethical ideals. At any rate, Christianity had always asserted its essential relation to the religion of Israel and to the nation, even though that relation might be variously defined within the movement and contain elements of unresolved ambiguity. Many believed, however, that the new policy of Paul, though he claimed it to be inherently involved in his commission to the Gentiles as given by Christ and as earlier acknowledged by the Jerusalem apostles themselves, undercut both the theoretic basis for and the practical polemic in the Jerusalem church's ministry. Paul's approach seemed to them to disprove his claim of continuity with Israel's faith, and for Jewish believers to acknowledge the legitimacy of such an approach was to bring their evangelistic endeavors under the same indictment in the eyes of their Jewish compatriots.

After considerable debate between Paul and Barnabas on the one side and the Judaizers who claimed the backing of the Jerusalem apostles on the other (Acts 15:1, 2), and realizing that this same debate was going on in the newly founded churches of southern Asia Minor, the Antioch church sent a delegation headed by Paul and Barnabas to Jerusalem to clarify matters with the apostles and elders there. The Antioch group came with news of the recent advance in the Christian mission, which they announced in Phoenicia and Samaria on their journey to Jerusalem in terms of "the conversion of the Gentiles" (Acts 15:3) – undoubtedly meaning the conversion of Gentiles on the basis of a direct ministry, for the presence of proselyte and God-fearing Gentile converts in the church was hardly news-worthy in the year A.D. 49. The delegation from Antioch was particularly concerned that the relation between the Jerusalem apostles' policy of expediency and the Judaizers' message based on principle be clarified, for outside of Jerusalem there was great confusion because of the Judaizers' habit of equating the two and thus claiming that they were backed by the whole of the Jerusalem church. The Jerusalem believers, for their part, were concerned that the implications involved in a direct approach to Gentiles receive a thorough airing, and that Paul and Barnabas be directly confronted with the impasse created for Christians in Jerusalem by their recently inaugurated policy. The issues, while closely related, seem to have boiled down to two: (1) the legitimacy of a direct ministry to Gentiles; and (2) the relation of a policy based on expediency to one founded on principle in the continued observance of the Mosaic law. The broader questions regarding the validity of a mission to Gentiles generally and the necessity for Jewish Christians to retain their relation to Jewish customs and institutions as a way of life seem to have been assumed as basically settled earlier, though, of course, there were undoubtedly some who felt that these issues had been thrown open to reevaluation. For the leaders at the Council, however, matters now concerned the explication of these commitments in the light of recent developments.

The Course of the Debate

In the debate that ensued within the Council, contributions to the discussion are recorded on the part of four groups or individuals. Some Christian Pharisees, evidently in defense of the Judaizers, set the problem by arguing: "It is necessary to circumcise them [Gentile converts], and to charge them to keep the law of Moses" (Acts 15:5). From the context of Luke's account, it seems that "necessary" meant both practically expedient and theologically required, since, for them, the issues were inextricably intertwined. In reply, Peter cited the conversion of Cornelius as indicating God's attitude toward the reception of Gentiles and as being a valid precedent to the Pauline policy (Acts 15:6-11). His argument, therefore, was to the effect that since the precedent for a direct ministry to Gentiles had been set within the Jewish Christian mission – though, of course, the Jerusalem church had never followed it out – Paul's practice in principle was not a revolutionary departure. Barnabas and Paul then told of their witness to Gentiles on that first missionary journey, dealing especially with how God gave His seal of approval through miracles and signs (Acts 15:12). Undoubtedly they also drew the parallel between the cases of Cornelius and Sergius Paulus. It is interesting to note that here the Acts account lists Barnabas first in naming the two apostles, since it was Barnabas who probably took the lead in explaining their activities in this situation where his word carried more weight with many than did that of Paul.

In summation, James concluded that on the theological issue of Gentile believers being related to the Mosaic law, "we should not trouble those of the Gentiles who turn to God" since the precedent had indeed been set within their own mission and the prophecy of Amos 9:11, 12 speaks expressly of Gentile inclusion (Acts 15:13-19). On the practical matter of the effect of the Pauline mission on the Christian witness in Jerusalem, and with some fear that Gentile converts might flaunt their liberty in disregard for the scruples of Jewish believers, he suggested that Gentile Christians be asked to keep themselves from (1) whatever is associated with idolatry, (2) immorality in all its forms,

(3) the eating of animals killed by strangulation, and (4) the eating of blood (Acts 15:20-29). And with James' advice the Church concurred, sending out Judas Barsabbas and Silas to explain the intent of the decision and the decree to believers at Antioch.

The Nature of the Decision

This was the type of decision consistent with the character and commitments of James and the Jerusalem apostles as portrayed elsewhere in Acts and Galatians. They could hardly have officially commended the Pauline policies. To do so would have meant for them the same fate as that suffered by the Hellenists. But neither could they be found resisting the general teaching of Scripture or the evident acceptance of the Gentiles by God expressed in miraculous and providential fashion. On the other hand, they could not overlook the practical demands involved in a ministry to Israel. Therefore, while they could not clasp the Gentile mission to their bosom or condone certain excesses which were rumored among the Jews to be prevalent in the Gentile world, they did disassociate themselves from the disruptive preaching of the Judaizers. And that was of immense importance to Paul and the furtherance of the Gentile mission.

When one considers the situation of the Jerusalem church in A.D. 49, the decision reached by the Jerusalem Christians must be considered one of the boldest and most magnanimous in the annals of church history. While still attempting to minister exclusively to the nation, they refused to impede the progress of that other branch of the Christian mission whose every success meant further oppression for them. All they asked was that in view of Jewish fears and sensibilities, the Gentile converts be instructed to abstain from certain practices which have been traditionally classified as the heinous vices of heathenism (cf. the so called Noachian commands of BT Sanhedrin 56b, evidently based upon Exod. 34:15, 16 and Lev. 16:1 - 18:30, and the listings of heinous ethical sins in Mishnah Aboth 5:11, BT Yoma 9b and BT Sanhedrin 74a). To such a decree Paul seems to have been happy to concede, since it stemmed from practical considerations of Jewish-Christian relationships and was not proposed as a basis for righteousness.

The effect of the decision made at Jerusalem was far-reaching.

In the first place, it freed the Gospel from any necessary entanglement with Judaism and the institutions of Israel, though without renouncing the legitimacy of a continued Christian expression and mission within those confines. Thus, the Gentile and Jewish missions of the church were able to progress side by side in the decade to follow without any essential conflict. Secondly, reactions to Paul within the Jerusalem church were clarified. It is possible that some of the Jewish believers were even more fixed in their enmity than before. But others of the Christian community at Jerusalem came to have more positive attitudes toward him, as seems to have been the case with John Mark (see discussion below). And some felt themselves happier in a Gentile ministry than at Jerusalem because of the deliberations of the Council, as was evidently true of Silas (Acts 15:27, 32, 34, 40). Thirdly, the decision made at the Council had the effect of permanently antagonizing the Jews. From this time forward, the Christian mission within the nation – and especially to Jews in and around Jerusalem – would face very rough sledding indeed. Paul said in Romans 11:28 to a predominantly Gentile audience, that the Jewish people, so far as concerns the Gospel, "are enemies of God, for your sake."

6

Second Missionary Journey

A further geographical advance in the proclamation of the Gospel occurred on the second missionary journey of Paul, for, although expecting at its inception to carry on the Gentile mission within the confines of Asia Minor, the apostle was directed into Macedonia and Achaia, regions of southeastern Europe. The account is given in Acts 15:36 - 18:22, with the journey spanning the years of approximately A.D. 49 to 52.

Two Missionary Teams

After the disruption caused by the Judaizers had been settled at Antioch, Paul desired to revisit the churches which had been founded on the first missionary journey. With this proposal Barnabas agreed. However, concerned for his cousin's spiritual development, he desired to take John Mark with them again. The request of Barnabas suggests that Mark's thinking regarding Paul and the Gentile mission had undergone a change of direction since his earlier defection, else he would never have wanted to involve himself in that which he had earlier renounced. The Jerusalem Council probably played a large part in his reevaluation of the issues, and now, wiser heads and hearts prevailing, he accepted the legitimacy of Paul's approach. But Paul did not care to have him along. Perhaps it was because of the report Mark gave when he returned to the congregation at Jerusalem that the Judaizing activity was stirred up against the mission originally. If this were so, Barnabas might have viewed Mark's presence on the team and his testimony to a change of mind as strategic in revisiting Christians who had known Mark. For Paul, however, the wound was too deep and the scars yet too tender to permit close association with one who had possibly, even though unwittingly, been a contributing factor in the original conflict. And while Mark may have experienced a real change of heart and mind, renouncing all Judaizing tendencies and professing to be solidly in support of the apostolic proclamation, Paul seems to have taken the position that the issues were too great and the welfare of the churches too important for them to risk his vacillations or to be reminded of earlier dissent within the party itself by his presence. With such a view, Barnabas found himself in complete disagreement, and in their "sharp contention," the two apostles found it best to part and carry on separate ministries. Thus, Barnabas went with Mark back to Cyprus, where the mission had originated and where Mark would be most effective, and Paul selected Silas as his new colleague, returning to the fields in Asia Minor (Acts 15:36-40).

Contention among Christians is never pleasant nor praise-worthy; and although the argument of Paul and Barnabas is described, there is no word condoning it or suggesting it as normative. Luke has simply portrayed his hero and the events of the time, "warts and all." Without attempting to minimize the seriousness of the matter, it must be noted, however, that the disagreement seems to have centered on the issues at stake, and did not, to judge by Paul's later remarks about the other persons involved, degenerate to the level of personal slander. On his third missionary journey Paul alluded to Barnabas in a letter to the Corinthians, classing him with himself as an apostle of highest rank (I Cor. 9:6). Later to Christians in the Lycus Valley of southern Asia Minor, who may have held some animosity toward Mark because of what they had heard regarding his early defection, Paul urged that John Mark be received should he come to them (Col. 4:10); and in his final letter prior to martyrdom, he instructed Timothy to bring Mark with him "for he is very useful in serving me" (II Tim. 4:11). Evidently even earnest and godly men of the highest order can differ, requiring a separation of ways; and while such a separation is never commended, neither does Scripture place a stigma upon either party when they separate apart from personal invective and attitudes of vindictiveness. In this case, of course, God used the difference to send out two missionary teams instead of one. And although Barnabas' ministry is not further detailed by Luke, one cannot take such an omission as a hint of disapproval. To judge by the later references of Paul to these two men, Barnabas and Mark evidently did excellent work in Cyprus. But Paul was Luke's hero, and with the Pauline ministry came the distinctive advances in the Gentile mission.

The choice of Silas as Paul's colleague was opportune, for he possessed a number of qualifications eminently suited to the Gentile mission as it went forward in the fifties of the first century. In the first place, of course, he was a leading Jerusalemite Christian able to represent sentiment as it existed in the church at Jerusalem (Acts 15:22, 27). He was also a prophet able to speak effectively to Gentiles (Acts 15:32); and from Paul's continued reference to him by his Roman name Silvanus (I Thess. 1:1; II Thess. 1:1), one may deduce that he was prepared to meet Gentiles on their own ground. In addition, he was a Roman citizen able to claim immunity from local persecution when necessary (Acts 16:37). As such, he fitted into and nicely complemented the mission of Paul. This easy association of Silas first with the Jerusalem apostles, then with Paul on the second and third missionary journeys, and finally with Peter again (I Pet. 5:12), is both an indication and an expression of the basic unity which existed between the two sections of early Christianity and their respective leaders.

The Ministry in Asia Minor

Leaving Syrian Antioch, Paul and Silas first visited the churches of Syria and Cilicia (Acts 15:41). Believers in these areas had probably been converted through the witness emanating from the church at Antioch, though some may have been won to the Lord by Paul during his earlier Tarsian ministry. Then traveling through the mountain passes forming the Cilician Gates, they came to Derbe and Lystra, and from there went on to the other churches of southern Asia Minor founded on the first missionary journey (Acts 16:1, 4). In all of the churches they announced the decision reached at the Jerusalem Council and gave instruction regarding the decrees formulated to relieve tensions between Jewish and Gentile believers, thereby strengthening the churches in the Christian faith. They also continued the proclamation of the Gospel, and many more were converted to Jesus Christ (Acts 16:4, 5).

At Lystra, Paul found the young man Timothy, a convert of the first journey, and asked that he join Silas and himself in their travels and ministry. Timothy's grandmother, Lois, and his mother, Eunice, were devout Jews who had become fervent Christians (Acts 16:1; II Tim. 1:5; 3:15). His father, however, was a Gentile who seems to have had no commitment to either Israel's God or the person of Christ. Since Timothy was a converted half-Jew, raised by his devout Jewish mother and grandmother and therefore would undoubtedly be considered a Jewish Christian by many, Paul had him circumcised so as not to offend the Jews unduly (Acts 16:3). While arguing strongly against the circumcision of Gentile converts, Paul never disputed the right — even the practical necessity in view of circumstances — for Jewish Christians to continue the practice of circumcision.

Many commentators have viewed Acts 16:6 as indicating that after revisiting the churches of southern Asia Minor, Paul and Silas went directly to the northern part of the province of Galatia and there established the churches to which the letter to the Galatians was later addressed. This theory grew up in the early patristic period at a time when the political boundaries of Galatia had been altered to conform to the ethnological grouping of Gauls living principally in the north. Thus they excluded the southern territory in which Antioch, Iconium, Lystra and Derbe were located, so that it did not occur to the fathers that the Galatian letter could have been written to churches in the south. The wording of Acts 16:6 in the Greek (wherein one article precedes two nouns of the same case connected by the conjunction "and") suggests, however, that the verse should read: "And when they had gone through the region of Phrygic-Galatia"; which would then specify a southern Galatian ministry, and give no support to a "North Galatian" thesis.

At the inception of the second journey, Paul seems to have intended extending the Gentile mission into the rich Roman province of Asia, in western Asia Minor. Having therefore strengthened the churches founded during his previous missionary endeavor, he sought to continue westward. But in some manner, perhaps through the prophetic Silas, he was "forbidden by the Holy Spirit to speak the word in Asia" (Acts 16:6b). He then decided to make for the large Roman cities on the coast of the Black Sea in the province of Bithynia, but again "the Spirit of Jesus did not allow them" (Acts 16:7). Not knowing precisely where they should minister, though aware that God had called them to move forward in the evangelization of the Gentiles, the missionary party turned toward Troas, located on the coast of the Aegean Sea. And at Troas, in a vision during the night, Paul saw a man of Macedonia who urged him to "come over to Macedonia and help us" (Acts 16:8, 9). Accepting this as direction from God, the apostles set their sights on the possibilities for evangelism in the cities beyond the Aegean to the west (Acts 16:10). It is at this point in the narrative that the third person pronoun changes to the first person, which has usually been taken to indicate that here Luke joined the missionary party – and which may also imply that Luke was employed by God in some manner in the "Macedonian vision" itself.

The Advance Into Europe

The mission to Macedonia began at Philippi, the leading city of the province and a Roman colony (Acts 16:11, 12). The city seems to have been devoid of any sizable Jewish population, for Paul had to seek out the devout worshipers of God on the sabbath day and found only women gathered by a river. Jewish law prescribes that wherever ten men who are heads of households reside, there a meeting place (synagogue) for the study of the Law should be built; otherwise the study of the Law in public session and corporate worship should take place in some clean area, a riverside being eminently appropriate. Here God opened the heart of Lydia, a seller of dyes and dyed cloth, to the Gospel; and after her baptism and the baptism of those in her household, she invited the missionary party to make her home their headquarters in the city (Acts 16:13-15). From this small beginning sprang the church at Philippi, whose members seem to have given Paul the most satisfaction and the least anxiety of all the churches in his care.

The ministry at Philippi was interrupted, however, at the cure of a clairvoyant slave girl, whose owners charged the apostles with interfering in what was for them a very profitable business. On the pretext that these traveling Jewish vagabonds were preaching an illegal religion which would ultimately undermine the peace and authority of Rome, the girl's owners were able to stir up the populace and local authorities against Paul and Silas. In the melee which followed, they were beaten and thrown into a dungeon under lock and key. At midnight, however, while "Paul and Silas were praying and singing hymns to God" (Acts 16:25), an earthquake occurred which shook open the doors of the prison and loosened the prisoners' shackles. Through such a manifestation of divine intervention, the jailer of the prison was converted and responded in kindness by washing the apostles' wounds. In the morning the local authorities ordered the police to release the apostles. But Paul and Silas demanded their rights to a public release as befitting Roman citizens; and after exhorting the infant church, left the city as requested by the officials (Acts 16:16-40). Luke may very well have remained behind at Philippi, for the personal pronoun in the narrative returns to the third person after this episode with the slave girl and its aftermath.

Coming to Thessalonica via Amphipolis and Apollonia, Paul and Silas were able to preach for three weeks in the synagogue with considerable success before the Jews incited a riot against them and their host, Jason (Acts 17:1-9). Their preaching focused on the death and resurrection of the Messiah according to prophecy and the identification of Jesus of Nazareth as the promised Messiah (Acts 17:3; cf. I Cor. 15:3-5). However, the charges laid against them were those of disturbing the peace and treason against the state (Acts 17:6, 7). Realizing the danger of the situation before the crisis reached its peak, the new converts of the city sent the missionary party away by night to Beroea (Acts 17:10). Paul accepted their intervention and aid. But from his first letter to them a few months later, we gather that he left with real fears for their personal safety and their steadfastness in the faith (I Thess. 2:17 - 3:5).

At Beroea, being "more noble than those in Thessalonica," the Jews of the synagogue were more concerned about the validity of Paul's claim that the Gospel was the fulfillment of the ancient Scriptures than about any dispute concerning his methods or the assertions of others as to the illegality of the Christian faith. Thus they gave him audience while they examined the biblical prophecies in the light of his proclamation. And, as a result, many Jews and Gentiles were converted to Christ (Acts 17:10-12). But the

Jews of Thessalonica came to Beroea and stirred up the mobs against him, with the result that Paul was again forced to flee. The opposition seems to have been only partially successful, however, since the Beroean Jews themselves took little active part in the persecution, and Silas and Timothy were able to remain to carry on the ministry in the city (Acts 17:13-15).

Paul's arrival at Athens in the province of Achaia appears to have been intended primarily as a refuge from persecution in Macedonia. But as he awaited the coming of Silas and Timothy from the north, he was stirred by the rampant idolatry of the city, and soon found himself compelled to present the claims of Christ in the synagogue to Jews and God-fearing Gentiles and in the market place to whosoever would listen (Acts 17:16, 17). As with Jeremiah, God's Word was in Paul's heart like a burning fire shut up in his bones, and he could not hold it in (Jer. 20:9).

Soon, however, certain adherents to the Epicurean and Stoic philosophies led him off, probably half in jest and half in derision, to the Areopagus (Acts 17:18-21); that is, to the Hill or Court of the god Ares (the Roman god Mars), the Greek god of war. The Council of the Areopagus in Roman times was an important tribunal in Athens, including among its many responsibilities the supervision of education in the city and the controlling of the many itinerant lecturers passing through. It was before this council that Paul was asked to speak, though the occasion was more an inquisition than an impartial inquiry. To those who gathered there, Paul spoke of the futility of idolatry, the revelation of God in nature, the universality of judgment, the progressive unfolding of God's redemptive program, and the climax of that redemption in God's raising Jesus from the dead (Acts 17:22-31). Many have attributed this address to the ingenuity of Luke, asserting that all of the speeches of Acts — and this one especially — are Thucydidean in nature; that is, they are free compositions by the author of Acts himself of what he thought would have been suitable to the speaker and to the occasion. But from one who professed himself willing to be "all things to all men" for the sake of the Gospel (I Cor. 9:20-22), there is nothing incongruous in such an address. On the contrary, it seems that Luke has here recorded but another instance of where Paul began on common ground with his hearers and attempted to lead them on to the person of Jesus Christ. However, in this instance the Pauline polemic is expressed in a different setting than previously presented.

Favorable responses to Paul's preaching at Athens were few. Most of the members of the Areopagus Council either mocked or remained noncommittal; though Dionysius, one of their number, believed. Also Damaris, who was a prominent woman of the city, and some others were converted (Acts 17:32-34). But no church seems to have been established at Athens. Many have suggested that Paul was plunged into despondency over the meager results, and that as he later reevaluated his attempt to speak philosophically to an educated audience, he forswore this strategy in favor of a simple pronouncement of the Gospel (I Cor. 1:20 - 2:5).

Now it is certainly probable that the apostle felt some discouragement over the fact that so few at Athens had come to Christ as a result of his ministry. But it must not be forgotten that some did respond! And it must be remembered that at this time Paul was preoccupied – indeed, almost sick with anxiety – over the state of the Thessalonian believers whom he had been forced to abandon to the threat of imminent persecution (I Thess. 2:17 - 3:5). As was true of his later inability to minister effectively at Troas because of his great concern for the church at Corinth (II Cor. 2:12, 13), or his earlier failure to evangelize Perga because of difficulties within the missionary party itself (see above, First Missionary Journey), Paul's anxiety regarding his Thessalonian converts must be viewed as to some extent preventing him from grasping fully the opportunities at hand. He was, after all, quite human; and as human, he too found his emotions to have an effect upon his spiritual effectiveness. In addition, it is likely that he was physically ill during much of this period, for he tells the Thessalonians that at Athens he repeatedly desired to visit them "but Satan hindered us" (I Thess. 2:18). This remark sounds very much like an allusion to an attack of his recurring sickness (cf. II Cor. 12:7-10).

Leaving Athens, Paul arrived alone at Corinth "in weakness and in much fear and trembling" (I Cor. 2:3). Here he stayed with Aquila and Priscilla, a Jewish couple recently banished from Rome by the Edict of Claudius in A.D. 49 which ordered the expulsion of all Jews from the capital because of disruptions within the Jewish community over a certain "Chrēstus" (Christ?).

Probably it is safe to assume that Aquila and his wife were Christians before coming to Corinth, since there is no record of their conversion through the preaching of Paul. And from them the apostle would have been able to learn much about the church at Rome of which they were members. As they were tentmakers by profession, he joined them in their trade during the course of the week while preaching in the synagogue every sabbath (Acts 18:1-4).

Shortly thereafter Silas and Timothy arrived in Corinth from Macedonia, bringing with them (1) a report on conditions in the church at Thessalonica (I Thess. 3:6), and (2) a monetary contribution from the church at Philippi (II Cor. 11:9; Phil. 4:14, 15). The news from Thessalonica was better than Paul dared to expect, and it greatly comforted and encouraged him (I Thess. 3:7-10). Silas and Timothy, however, also told about a campaign of slander against Paul originating from outside the church (I Thess. 2:3-6) and of some perplexity within concerning the return of Christ (I Thess. 4:13 - 5:11). The money from Philippi enabled him to devote his full time to the preaching of the Gospel, for, as Acts 18:5 reads literally, now "Paul held himself to the word."

It was in response to the report from Thessalonica that Paul wrote First Thessalonians, in which are interwoven (1) commendation for growth, zeal and fidelity, (2) encouragement in the face of local persecution, (3) defense of his motives against hostile attack, (4) teaching regarding holiness of life, (5) instruction as to the coming of the Lord, and (6) exhortation to steadfastness and patience. Some weeks later, on learning of continued confusion at Thessalonica regarding the return of Christ and the believer's relation to that blessed hope, he wrote Second Thessalonians. In this second letter, while acknowledging that the Church lives in eager expectation of the Lord's return, Paul insists that imminency must not be construed to mean immediacy, but rather it is the basis for steadfastness and dogged persistence. The two letters to the Thessalonian Christians were written about A.D. 50 - 51.

The ministry of Paul at Corinth followed the typical pattern of an original proclamation in the synagogue, and then a direct witness to Gentiles. This time after expulsion by the Jews he made his headquarters in the home of Titus Justus, whose house stood next to the synagogue (Acts 18:5-7). One of the first converts at Corinth was Crispus, who was then the ruler of the synagogue. He was followed by many others of the city who believed and were baptized (Acts 18:8; I Cor. 1:14); though Paul baptized very few of them himself (I Cor. 1:14-16). When Gallio was appointed the proconsul of the province of Achaia, the Jews made a concentrated attack against Paul on the charge that, as they said, "This man is persuading men to worship God contrary to the law." What they meant, evidently, was that Paul's gospel was against the law of Rome which permitted only one religion per recognized unit of people, and that the Gospel was against the law of Moses, as they understood it. Gallio, however, saw the issue as only an intramural squabble of Judaism, and refused to take any official action on it (Acts 18:12-17). Paul was therefore given a free hand in Corinth to continue his preaching, and he remained in the city for over eighteen months (Acts 18:11, 18). A Latin inscription found at Delphi puts it beyond doubt that Gallio was proconsul of Achaia in A.D. 52, and that probably he began his two-year term of office in July of A.D. 51, which corresponds roughly with the portrayal of Paul's ministry at Corinth as given in Acts.

Leaving Corinth for the trip to Syria, the missionary party was accompanied by Aquila and Priscilla as far as Ephesus. At Ephesus Paul had some opportunity to speak in the synagogue, but felt it necessary to postpone any further evangelization in the city until a later time. At Cenchreae, just prior to his arrival at Ephesus, he had taken upon himself some kind of vow; and although we are told nothing further as to its nature, it seems to have been hurrying him on toward Jerusalem (Acts 18:18-21). Finally landing at Caesarea after a long sea voyage, he went to Jerusalem to greet the Christians there and then returned north to Antioch of Syria (Acts 18:22).

7

Third Missionary Journey

The third missionary journey of Paul was principally given to an extended ministry at Ephesus, the city the apostle apparently hoped to reach at the inception of his second journey and which showed much promise for the preaching of the Gospel in his short visit not more than a year before. Acts 18:23 - 21:16 gives the account in very abbreviated fashion, though a few additional details may be supplied from his letters. In all, the third missionary journey lasted from approximately A.D. 53 through 58.

Extended Ministry at Ephesus

After revisiting the churches in "the region of Galatia and Phrygia, strengthening all the disciples" (Acts 18:23), the missionary party came to Ephesus. The city had two important assets upon which it relied for its life and vitality. The first was its position as a center of trade, for Ephesus was an important seaport on the Aegean Sea, linking overseas ports with the cities of the Roman province of Asia. But because of the gradual silting up of its harbor caused by the flow of the Little Meander River into it, the city's significance as a center of commerce was beginning to wane in the days of Paul. Efforts had repeatedly been made to improve the harbor, and in A.D. 65 a large-scale attempt was undertaken, but the efforts either failed or provided only temporary relief.

The second factor of importance at Ephesus was the worship of Artemis (Diana), the multiple-breasted goddess of fertility whose temple was one of the seven wonders of the world. The relation of Artemis of Ephesus to the Greek goddess Artemis is exceedingly vague, for although in their distinctive characteristics they were quite different, in the popular mind they were probably often equated. With the decline in commerce, however, the prosperity of the city became more heavily dependent upon the tourists and pilgrims drawn by the temple and cult of Artemis. At the time of Paul's arrival, the people of Ephesus, while surrounded by signs of past opulence and still able to enjoy the fruits of that wealth, were becoming conscious of the precariousness of their position as a commercial and political center of Asia and were turning more toward the temple in support of their economy.

On reaching Ephesus, Paul met twelve men who had been baptized "into John's baptism" but who gave no evidence of being truly Christian. When they heard the Gospel of Jesus Christ, they were baptized "in the name of the Lord Jesus" (Acts 19:1-7). The account is somewhat difficult to interpret, primarily because it is so brief. Probably, however, (prior to their meeting with Paul) these twelve may be considered to have been sectarians who in some sense thought of John the Baptist as the apex of God's revelation in this period of redemptive history — perhaps even as the Messiah Himself. The polemic of John 1:19-34 and 2:22-36 against anyone thinking of the Baptist as superior to Jesus, together with the emphasis upon "one Lord, one faith, one baptism" in Ephesians 4:5, suggests that a John the Baptist sect existed within Jewish Christian circles in Asia in the first century (assuming, of course, the Ephesian connections of the fourth gospel and the letter to the Ephesians). And as in any such group — especially before issues have become solidified — some undoubtedly venerated John the Baptist, yet looked forward to greater fulfillment, whereas others were prepared to go no further than the Baptist in their devotion — even to elevating him higher than Jesus in their esteem.

Apollos seems to have been of the first variety, for, although from a John the Baptist group, he had been taught "accurately" and needed only that Aquila and Priscilla teach him "more accurately" (Acts 18:24-28). It would seem, then, that Apollos was never considered a sectarian, "though he knew only the baptism of John," since that baptism was considered by him as a prolegomenon to the reception of God's Messiah; and when instructed regarding further events and implications, he readily accepted. Of interest in his case is the fact that there is no mention of his baptism in the name of Christ. It is, of course, precarious to argue from silence; though perhaps, as seems to have been the case with the disciples of Jesus themselves, John's baptism was accepted as Christian baptism when received as a prolegomenon to Christ. The twelve whom Paul met, however, while maintaining some relation to Jewish Christianity generally, were evidently those who considered the Baptist as the focus of their devotion and as such were sectarians. Despite their claims, Paul preached Jesus to them as he would to any Jew. And upon their conversion, he baptized them in the name of the Lord Jesus.

The ministry in Ephesus lasted almost three years, and is recorded in very brief fashion in Acts 19. One could wish to know more than what is told, but one can hardly find fault with what has been given him for that reason. For three months Paul spoke openly in the synagogue, "arguing and pleading about the kingdom of God" (Acts 19:8). He was speaking to those who had earlier given him a favorable reception (Acts 18:19-21), and the time of his ministry there was one of the longest ever afforded him in any of the synagogues of Judaism. When opposition arose within the synagogue, however, he moved to the lecture hall of Tyrannus, where he continued his preaching for another two years (Acts 19:9, 10). During this period, "the word of the Lord grew and prevailed mightily," accompanied by many miracles, exorcisms, and renunciations of magical works (Acts 19:11-20). And from Ephesus, probably by converts of Paul, the Gospel was carried out to the residents of the province of Asia so that all were made aware of Paul's message and other churches were founded (Acts 19:10; cf. Col. 1:7; 2:1, and the Letters of Ignatius). Then after sending Timothy and Erastus as his envoys to Macedonia and Achaia, Paul stayed for a while longer at Ephesus (Acts 19:21, 22).

At the close of Paul's ministry in the city, a riot broke out against him and his preaching. The Gospel had turned many away from the idolatry of the Artemis cult, with the result that the economy of the city as a pilgrim center was being affected. Demetrius and his fellow silversmiths had had a profitable business in making statuettes of the goddess for the tourist trade, but when Paul's message began to touch their pocketbooks, they attempted to instigate a revival on behalf of Artemis and to turn the people against the Christian missioners (Acts 19:23-28). They dragged Gaius and Aristarchus, two companions of Paul, into the large theater, and for two hours led the crowd in frenzied cheering and shouting for Artemis of Ephesus (Acts 19:29-34). The Jewish community tried to disassociate itself from the Christians, and sent one of its number, Alexander, onto the podium for this purpose. But to the idolatrous mob, Jews were as insufferable as Christians on the point in question, for both proclaimed an invisible deity and rejected all idols; and Alexander was shouted down (Acts 19:33, 34). Paul wanted to enter the theater to plead before the assembly himself, but the crowd was in such an angry mood that the Christians and some of the local authorities prevented him (Acts 19:30, 31). Finally the town clerk was able to disperse the people with the argument that the prestige of the city, in which they all were interested, could hardly be enhanced in the eyes of Rome by a riot, and that therefore any complaint raised by Demetrius and his craftsmen should be brought before the legally constituted authorities (Acts 19:35-41). His work being done, and conscious that his presence would only arouse further antagonism, Paul and his party left for Macedonia (Acts 20:1).

Undoubtedly, Luke has omitted a great deal regarding the persecutions that arose at the end of Paul's ministry in Ephesus. Although there is no evidence that the apostle was ever imprisoned during this time by the sentence of some kangaroo court, as some have postulated, his later allusions to events in Asia indicate that the difficulties were intense and traumatic. Certainly the statement of First Corinthians 15:32 regarding having "fought with beasts at Ephesus," which is likely a metaphor for extreme oppression (note the accompanying "I die every day" of verse thirty-one), suggests something of the grievous nature of this experience. And probably his references in Romans 16:3, 4 to Aquila and Priscilla having risked their necks for his life and in Second Corinthians 1:8-11 to his having been so crushed that he despaired of life have events in the Ephesian ministry in mind.

Continued Contact With Churches

During the third missionary journey, Paul had prolonged and complex dealings with the Christians of Corinth. While at Ephesus he wrote a letter to them on the subject of separation from the ungodly (I Cor. 5:9, 10), which letter is now no longer extant or is partially preserved (as often suggested) in Second Corinthians 6:14 - 7:1. In reply he received a letter from certain members of the church (I Cor. 7:1) seeking his advice on matters concerning marriage and its problems at Corinth, food that had previously been dedicated to idols, the decorum of women in worship, the observance of the Lord's Supper, spiritual gifts, and possibly the significance and nature of the resurrection. At about the same time he had some visitors from Corinth, whom he identifies as "Chloe's people" (I Cor. 1:11), who told of deep and bitter divisions within the church; and from rumors widely circulating (I Cor. 5:1) he knew that there existed blatant immorality and also litigations between members in the public lawcourts. To deal with all this, the apostle wrote in strong pastoral tones a second letter which we know as First Corinthians. The problems at Corinth then seem to have taken the course of opposition to Paul's authority and criticism of his doctrine, and he was forced to make a "painful visit" to the city in an attempt to settle matters within the church (II Cor. 2:1; 12:14; 13:1). This visit of which he speaks in Second Corinthians is quite obscure, not being mentioned by Luke in Acts; and it may or may not have been conducted on his behalf by Timothy and Erastus (Acts 19:22) or Titus (II Cor. 12:17, 18; see also 2:13; 7:6, 13, 14; 8:6, 16, 23). Nevertheless, the fact that it is spoken of as a "painful visit" and that Paul must continue to rebuke, suggests that it was not thoroughly successful. His opponents, it seems, even taunted him with being humble when face to face with them, but bold when away (II Cor. 10:1). They said, "His letters are weighty and strong, but his bodily presence is weak, and his speech of no account" (II Cor. 10:10).

Leaving Ephesus, Paul moved north to Troas. But being agitated about conditions at Corinth, and not finding Titus awaiting him there from whom he hoped to learn about the state of affairs at Corinth, he moved on to Macedonia without any further witness in Troas (II Cor. 2:12, 13). In Macedonia (probably at Philippi) he received Titus' report, and sent as his earnest response to the triumphs and continuing difficulties at Corinth the letter known as Second Corinthians. Many have proposed that Second Corinthians 10 - 13, the "Severe Letter," preceded the writing of Second Corinthians 1 - 9 (with or without 6:14 - 7:1), the "Conciliatory Letter." Although this is possible, there is little that requires such a view.

One activity which especially concerned Paul on his third missionary journey was the gathering of a collection of money for the relief of the impoverished believers of Jerusalem, and regarding this, he instructed his Gentile churches in Galatia, Asia, Macedonia and Achaia (Rom. 15:25-32; I Cor. 16:1-4; II Cor. 8 and 9). It was a great act of kindness, comparable to that undertaken by the Antioch church much earlier. But more than this, Paul seems to have viewed it as a symbol of unity which would help his Gentile converts realize their debt to the mother church at Jerusalem and give Jewish Christians an appreciation of the vitality of the faith existent in the Gentile churches. It was during this third missionary journey that Illyricum to the west was evangelized as well (Rom. 15:19), though whether Paul himself made an excursion into the area or converts from Macedonia were the evangelists is uncertain.

After spending some time in the Macedonian churches, Paul went to Corinth where he stayed three months (Acts 20:2, 3). One could wish to know more about this three-month visit and Paul's relations with the church, especially in light of his earlier correspondence, but the account of Acts is silent.

While at Corinth, and before his final trip to Jerusalem, the apostle wrote his letter to the Christians of Rome (Rom. 15:17-33). The Greek world in the eastern part of the empire had been evangelized (Rom. 15:19, 23) — the flame had been kindled and the fire was spreading — and Paul desired to transfer his ministry to the Latin world, going as far west as Spain (Rom. 15:24). Evidently he expected the Roman church to serve as his base of operations, much as the church at Antioch in Syria had served previously. He had hoped earlier to go directly to Rome from Achaia, but his presence was essential at Jerusalem if the Gentile contribution were to carry the full meaning he wanted it to have (Rom. 15:22-32). Therefore, in place of a personal visit, as preparation for his future coming to them, and to declare the righteousness of God, Paul sent this formal letter to Christians he had never met in Rome.

The letter itself is the longest and most systematic of Paul's writings, and more a comprehensive exposition of the Gospel than a letter as such. Some have suggested, in fact, that the body of the work may have been composed by the apostle earlier in his ministry and circulated among his Gentile churches as something of a missionary tractate giving a résumé of his message, and when directed to Rome had been supplemented by the personal elements of chapters fifteen and sixteen. Such a view would go far toward explaining the uncertainties within the early church regarding the relation of the final two chapters to the rest of the writing, the absence of "in Rome" at 1:7 and 1:15 in some minor manuscripts, and the presence of the two doxologies at 15:33 and 16:27.

A plot to kill Paul on the Jewish pilgrim ship sailing for Jerusalem was uncovered at Corinth, and he redirected his journey back through Macedonia by land (Acts 20:3). He was accompanied by the representatives from the churches: Sopater of Beroea, Aristarchus and Secundus of Thessalonica, Gaius of Derbe, Timothy of Lystra, and Tychicus and Trophimus from the Asian churches (Acts 20:4). All of the main centers in the Gentile mission were represented, except Philippi and Corinth. It is probable, however, that Luke served as the representative of Philippi, and Paul himself might have been delegated by the Corinthian congregation as their representative – though this omission may be taken as evidence of continued strained relations and difficulties at Corinth.

At Philippi Paul celebrated the Passover while his Gentile associates went ahead to Troas (Acts 20:5, 6). Later at Troas he held a midnight Eucharist and preached until morning, much to the physical discomfort of the young man Eutychus who fell in his sleep from a third-floor window ledge (Acts 20:6-12). Paul's desire was to be in Jerusalem on the day of Pentecost (Acts 20: 16), and thus he wanted to sail as fast as possible around Asia Minor without any delay in revisiting his churches on the way. At Miletus, however, he called the Ephesian elders to him, giving them one final sermon of exhortation (Acts 20:17-38). From there Paul sailed to Cyprus, Tyre and Ptolemais, touching at various smaller ports on the way, and then journeyed by land to Caesarea.

8

Imprisonments and Martyrdom

The importance of the period of the Pauline imprisonments in Palestine and Rome is somewhat signaled by the fact that Luke devotes one-fourth of his account of the early church to it, Acts 21 through 28. This does not mean, of course, that the defenses, imprisonments and martyrdom of Paul are more important than any other event in the history of the early church. Luke's proportions in writing are dependent upon his purposes; and while various kerygmatic, catechetical and even conciliatory motifs are intertwined in his work, he also has an apologetic purpose which lays heavy emphasis upon the Pauline trials and defenses. But Luke's proportions do suggest that this period in the apostle's life and ministry must be considered more than simply the finale to a successful career, and has significance of itself. The period covers a wide expanse of time, perhaps as long as a decade: beginning with the apostle's arrest in Jerusalem about A.D. 58; including a two-year confinement at Caesarea from A.D. 58 through 60, a trip of some months by sea to Rome from late A.D. 60 to the spring of 61, a two-year imprisonment at Rome from A.D. 61 through 63; and probably incorporating a period of release and subsequent ministry from A.D. 63 through 66, with a second Roman incarceration and final martyrdom under Nero in A.D. 67.

Circumstances in Palestine

On reaching Tyre in Syria, and again on coming to Caesarea in Palestine, Paul was strongly urged by the Christians of those cities not to go to Jerusalem, for they had been told by the Holy Spirit that imprisonment and afflictions awaited him there (Acts

21:4, 11, 12). At first glance it might appear that the apostle was being ordered by the Spirit not to proceed any further in his plans and that his determination to go on was in disobedience to that direction. The preposition "through" of Acts 21:4, however, may just as properly be understood to signify that the Spirit's message about what would befall the apostle was *the occasion* for their urging as that the Spirit himself was *the agent.* Also, as with Agabus' earlier prophecy where the fact of the famine was revealed and the church took action in response (Acts 11:27-30), the Caesarean believers' urging is probably to be understood as based upon the revelation of disastrous events ahead and not necessarily the revelation itself. Paul's determination to go to Jerusalem was the fruit of an inward spiritual constraint which could not be set aside (Acts 19:21; 20:22). He was well aware that his reception at Jerusalem could be less than cordial. It was natural that on learning something of the difficulties ahead, his friends should try to dissuade him. Yet when he could not be persuaded, and evidently after some explanation on his part, their reply was "the will of the Lord be done" (Acts 21:14).

At Caesarea Paul stayed "for some days" (Acts 21:10). The timing of his stopovers prior to his arrival at Caesarea had been largely dependent upon the shipping schedules, and thus he remained at Tyre, for example, for seven days while the boat was being unloaded (Acts 21:3, 4). But at Caesarea he seems to have been able to arrange his own schedule. For a man in a hurry to get to Jerusalem, such a delay appears somewhat strange and raises the question as to why there was a break in the journey here. Of course he might have wanted to rest after the strenuous trip from Corinth to Philippi by land, Philippi to Ptolemais by sea, and then Ptolemais to Caesarea by land again. And certainly he would have found a congenial welcome among the Caesarean believers. More to the point, however, was his desire to be in Jerusalem on the day of Pentecost (Acts 20:16) — not just to arrive in Jerusalem as early as possible, but to arrive at what he believed to be the strategic moment. Thus his stay at Caesarea was probably in large measure a waiting for the proper moment for entrance into Jerusalem. And when that came, he was escorted by some of the Caesarean believers into the

Holy City and given lodging in the home of Mnason, one of the early believers whose native country was Cyprus (Acts 21:16).

The day following their arrival in Jerusalem, Paul and the representatives from the Gentile churches met with James and the Jerusalem elders. At this meeting they rehearsed all that God had done in the Gentile mission and undoubtedly presented the contribution which they had brought (Acts 21:17-19). They were cordially enough received, though James and the elders were concerned about the reactions of many Jewish believers in Jerusalem to Paul's presence, since they had heard that he taught Jews in the Diaspora to forsake the Law. Evidently religious fervor and ritual had become considerably more rigid within the Jerusalem church since Paul's "famine visit," possibly, as some have suggested, because of the conversion of many former Essenes who had been accustomed to blending an inward piety with a very strict observance of the Law. And though James and the Jerusalem apostles never went on record as favoring such a development, they seem to have been hard-pressed to control it. Thus they suggested to Paul that in an endeavor to alleviate the fears engendered by the malicious rumors about him, he publicly show his respect for Jewish customs and piety by joining in the temple rites of Nazirite purification about to be performed by four Jewish Christians and by paying the expenses for the five of them. He agreed to do this, for, while insisting that Gentile believers were free from the Jewish customs and cultus, he found no fault with Jewish Christians who chose to express their faith in this manner (Acts 21:20-26). As a matter of fact, he himself continued to live the scrupulous life of a Pharisee during his missionary travels even while arguing for the freedom of Gentiles (Acts 23:6; 26:5).

The strategy, however, proved hardly successful – probably nothing could have really conciliated those whose minds were already deeply prejudiced against him. Seeing Paul in the temple, fanatical Jews from the province of Asia instigated a riot under the pretense that he had brought Trophimus, the Gentile representative from Ephesus, into the court of Israel. In the tumult, Paul might have been killed had it not been for the intervention of the Roman tribune Claudius Lysias and his soldiers from the garrison quartered at the Castle of Antonia, located to the north, adjacent to the temple precincts. The howling mob, disappointed in its efforts to do away with the apostle, crowded about shouting, "Away with him!" (Acts 21:27-36).

As he was about to be dragged into the Roman fortress, Paul requested permission of the tribune to address the crowd. Recognizing him to be able and earnest, the tribune permitted it (Acts 21:37-40). Raising his hands for silence, Paul spoke to the people from the castle steps in Aramaic, and they listened intently to his account of his life in Judaism and his conversion to Christianity. But when he mentioned his commission to minister to the Gentiles, the tumult broke out afresh (Acts 22:1-22). Thereupon the tribune hurried the apostle into the garrison and gave orders that he should be examined under the lash in order to get from him the truth concerning the reason for the outcry. By appealing to his Roman citizenship, however, Paul was spared scourging and was released from his chains (Acts 22:23-29).

The next day, in an endeavor to learn what Judaism had against the man, the tribune brought Paul to trial before the Jewish Sanhedrin. But that body could come to no decision, thanks to a stratagem on Paul's part to divide his enemies, and the apostle was returned to the Antonian castle (Acts 22:30 - 23:10). Then more than forty men vowed to kill Paul by ambush, and arranged with the Jewish leaders to ask for his return to the Sanhedrin for further questioning. But Paul's nephew heard of the plot and managed to warn both him and the Roman tribune (Acts 23:12-22). Believing the lad's story to be plausible, Claudius Lysias, the tribune, sent Paul by night under heavy escort to Caesarea, where in the custody of the Roman procurator Felix he would be safe from local insurrectionists and could be examined further (Acts 23:23-35). At Caesarea Paul had two formal hearings before Felix, and was called in a number of times for private conversations. But Felix, unwilling to antagonize the Jews by acquitting him, though also not prepared to commit an injustice by condemning him, procrastinated in disposing of the case. Thus Paul was confined to Herod's prison in Caesarea for two full years, though with freedom of movement within his place of confinement. He was also allowed to receive visitors (Acts 24:1-27).

There are many things one would like to know about this two-year imprisonment. For instance, how was the apostle supported during this time? Felix thought that he was a man of some wealth and backing (Acts 24:26), but on what basis did he suppose this? How cordial were Paul's relations with the Jerusalem Christians and their leaders after his imprisonment? How cordial were his contacts with the Caesarean believers, or with other groups of Christians in the vicinity? What happened to Silas? Presumably he was not imprisoned with Paul; he appears only once again in the New Testament, and that in connection with Peter (I Pet. 5:12). What were Timothy and Luke doing during this period? What happened to the rest of those who represented the Gentile churches in Jerusalem? A host of other questions arise, all of which lend themselves to various speculations. But these interests are evidently not those of Luke in writing his history, or of Paul in his letters, and nothing is said on these points. Some have suggested that several of Paul's extant letters were written while he was in prison at Caesarea, but internal evidence points rather to their composition during his subsequent Roman imprisonment.

When Felix was replaced by Porcius Festus, the Jews appealed to the new Roman procurator to have Paul returned to Jerusalem for trial under Jewish jurisdiction. But Festus told them to send their representatives to Caesarea, and when they came he found that they were unable to substantiate their charges (Acts 25:1-8).

Nevertheless, wishing to conciliate the Jews, Festus asked Paul if he were willing to go to Jerusalem to be tried. Paul had waited through two years of Felix's procrastinations, and now saw that justice under Festus would be just as remote. Therefore, as a Roman citizen, he appealed for judgment to be given by the emperor's court in Rome (Acts 25:9-11). Never before had Paul made such an appeal; nor would he have thought to make such an appeal, for release from the possibility of Jewish jurisdiction was really to place himself outside of all Jewish privileges as well – which included free access to the synagogue. But his situation in Palestine was going from bad to worse, caught as he was between Jewish hatred and Roman vacillation, and to argue his case in person in Caesar's court would provide him with an opportunity of proclaiming the Gospel before the most exalted audience in the world. Thus, as Festus declared: "You have appealed to Caesar; to Caesar you shall go" (Acts 25:12).

Before arrangements were completed to send him, however,

Herod Agrippa II and his sister Bernice visited Festus at Caesarea to welcome him to his new post. Agrippa was the titular king of the Jews, and Festus turned to him in an endeavor to determine what charges he should lay against Paul in sending him to Caesar (Acts 25:13-27). Thus Paul was given opportunity to speak before Agrippa, and in so doing delivered one of his most famous addresses (Acts 26:1-23). Festus, lately come from Rome, was sure that Paul was mad in speaking of visions and the resurrection of Jesus. Agrippa, though in a better position to evaluate Paul's evidence, could only rather superciliously ask whether the apostle was trying to convert him (Acts 26:24-29). Both agreed, however, that justice would have demanded Paul's release. But in appealing to Caesar the apostle had set his own course (Acts 26:30-32).

Rome at Last

The voyage to Rome is narrated in the first person plural, suggesting that Luke traveled with Paul on the trip. Probably Timothy embarked as well, and there may have been others also attending the apostle (Acts 27:1). Leaving Caesarea in the early autumn of A.D. 60, the ship encountered a fierce storm and became wrecked on the island of Malta (Acts 27:9 - 28:10). Setting out again the next spring in another vessel, Paul and his captors finally landed at Puteoli in the bay of Naples (Acts 28:11-13). There they stayed with the native Christians for seven days; and then went on by land to Rome, where a delegation of Roman Christians met Paul as he approached the city along the Appian Way (Acts 28:14, 15).

Paul was in Rome at last, fulfilling his great ambition to visit the capital of the empire. But now he had come not as a traveling evangelist, but as Caesar's prisoner awaiting trial. Guarded by a soldier, to whom he was manacled by a chain, he was kept in custody under house arrest. Yet he was free to receive visitors, and during the period of his confinement at Rome he carried on an extensive and effective ministry through emissaries (Acts 28:17-31).

Shortly after reaching Rome, Paul came into contact with three individuals who had come from the provinces of Asia and Macedonia, and who became the occasion for most of his extant letters from prison. One whom he met was Epaphras, who either visited

Paul in prison or was actually imprisoned with him (Philemon 23). Epaphras seems to have been the one who founded the church at Colosse (Col. 1:7; 4:12, 13), probably having been himself a convert of Paul during the Ephesian ministry. In meeting Paul at Rome, Epaphras told of conditions in the church at Colosse: of faith and love among the Christians (Col. 1:4, 8), but also of a heresy threatening to pervert the Gospel. And regarding this problem Paul wrote his letter to the Colossians, sending it by Tychicus in the company of Onesimus about A.D. 61, or perhaps in early A.D. 62.

From Paul's response to the problem, it seems probable that the heresy at Colosse was built upon some type of syncretistic and dualistic religious philosophy which taught that since the world of matter is defiled and intrinsically opposed to God, man must seek true knowledge and union with deity in some higher sphere of the nonmaterial. Specifically, this means that the incarnation of our Lord and His work on the cross are either to be rejected or to be viewed as an inferior first step toward full reconciliation with God.

In his answer, Paul does not minimize the humanity and the sacrifice of Christ, though these were the points at which offense was taken. Rather he glories in the incarnation and the cross, for by them God has effected man's redemption (Col. 1:20-22). The teaching of dualistic gnosticism states that the more deeply God penetrates the universe of the material the less revelatory become His actions and the more man must seek higher for redemptive knowledge. Contrary to this, Paul proclaimed the cosmic Christ in whom all the fullness of the Godhead dwells and in whom the believer finds complete redemption and reconciliation (Col. 1:15-22; 2:9, 10).

Another person whom Paul met at Rome was Onesimus, a slave under bondage to Philemon of Colosse. He had robbed his master and fled to Rome, undoubtedly hoping to become anonymous in the great city. Perhaps through Epaphras, Onesimus had come into contact with Paul. At any rate, Onesimus was brought to Christ by Paul and proved very helpful to the apostle while he was in prison. Having persuaded Onesimus to return to his master, Paul wrote the letter to Philemon urging him to receive his servant back as a "beloved brother in the Lord" (Philem. 16). An exquisite sense of humor seen in the play on the name Onesimus ("profitable," "useful") relieves the intensity of the letter and strengthens its appeal.

Interestingly, the apostle's approach to this crucial social problem of his day was to work from a "Christ consciousness" in the individual to a "Christian consciousness" in society. In so doing he planted the seeds for the ultimate abolition of the system of slavery. From the references to Tychicus and Onesimus in Colossians 4:7-9, and the comparable greetings in both epistles (Col. 4:10-17, Philem. 1, 2, 23, 24), it can be deduced that both the letter to the Colossians and the one to Philemon were written and sent at the same time. Carried by the same Tychicus (Eph. 6:21), and probably composed in the same period, was the letter to the Ephesians, which probably was originally intended as something of a circular letter to the churches of Asia Minor.

The third of the three members from his churches in the East whom Paul met in Rome was Epaphroditus. Having aided the apostle financially at least twice before (Phil. 4:15, 16), and hearing of his arrest and imprisonment, the Philippian church sent Epaphroditus with a gift. Perhaps he was also to serve Paul personally during his confinement, and may even have been sent in time to be among those who welcomed the apostle to Rome. But Epaphroditus became seriously ill while he was with Paul, and news of his condition eventually reached Philippi. In the letter to the Philippians, Paul wrote to thank the Christians there for their financial aid (Phil. 4:10-19). Also he wrote to commend Epaphroditus, their messenger to him, against any possible criticism that he had not completed his task (Phil. 2:25-30). He took the occasion to explain regarding his present circumstances, to exhort to steadfastness, unity and humility, and to warn against the Judaizers. Since he alludes to an approaching determination of his case (Phil. 1:20ff) and expresses his hope to visit Philippi shortly (Phil. 2:24), the letter may be taken to have been written from Rome toward the end of his first imprisonment, about A.D. 63.

For two full years Paul was confined at Rome (Acts 28:30), which was the period of time prescribed by Roman law as the limit a prisoner might be held after appeal to the emperor's court should there be no prosecution of the case. At this point Luke's narrative in Acts comes to an end, with the implication to be drawn that either the defendant was tried, found guilty, and summarily executed, or that the Jewish plaintiffs allowed the case to go by default and he was released. Although he was unable to be certain about the outcome, the apostle expected the latter (Philem. 22; Phil. 2:24); and there is little reason to believe otherwise. Two full years of imprisonment in Rome may seem to have been an unnecessary waste of time. But the apostle, in writing to the Philippians just prior to his release, declared: "I want you to know, brethren, that what has happened to me has really served to advance the gospel, so that it has become known throughout the whole praetorian guard and to all the rest that my imprisonment is for Christ; and most of the brethren have been made confident in the Lord because of my imprisonment, and are much more bold to speak the word of God without fear" (Phil. 1:12-14).

Subsequent Ministry and Death

What happened to Paul at the end of the two-year imprisonment in Rome is not told. Luke may have intended to write a sequel to his accounts of the life and work of Jesus and the advance of the Gospel in the East, which would have told of the advance of the Gospel into the western portion of the empire. But whatever his hopes may have been, there is obviously no such record extant. The closest approach to such an account is in the letter of Clement of Rome to the Corinthians, written about A.D. 96, wherein the following epitaph appears: "By reason of jealousy and strife, Paul by his example pointed out the prize of patient endurance. After that he had been seven times in bonds, had been driven into exile, had been stoned, had preached in the East and in the West, he won the noble renown which was the reward of his faith, having taught righteousness unto the whole world and having reached the farthest bounds of the West; and when he had borne his testimony before the rulers, so he departed from the world and went unto the holy place, having been found a notable pattern of patient endurance" (I Clement 5). Since the Pastoral Epistles allude to experiences of Paul which cannot be fitted into the narrative of Acts and mention a number of individuals not appearing in the accounts of the missionary journeys, it has often been postulated that after his release from prison the apostle continued his evangelistic work in the eastern portion of the empire (at least in lands surrounding the Aegean Sea) and perhaps even fulfilled his long cherished desire to visit Spain. And since Second Timothy speaks of him as in prison, it is further suggested that he was rearrested about A.D. 67, and, according to tradition, beheaded at Rome by order of Nero.

Assuming such hypotheses to be at least approximately true, Paul wrote the letters of First Timothy and Titus during the period of release in A.D. 63 to 66 and that of Second Timothy just prior to his death in A.D. 67.

In his first letter to Timothy, he seeks to encourage his young colleague in his pastoral responsibilities at Ephesus. He exhorts Timothy to deal decisively with certain false teachers and gives instruction regarding the qualifications for leaders and the treatment of various members in the church. In his letter to Titus, the minister of the church at Crete, he again admonishes concerning pastoral duties and deals with (1) qualifications for leaders in the church, (2) the need to oppose false doctrine, (3) treatment of various classes of members in the fellowship, and (4) proper attitudes for believers in a pagan society. Second Timothy is chronologically later than the other Pastoral Epistles, and breathes a different atmosphere. Whereas in First Timothy and Titus the apostle is free to make plans and move about at will, in Second Timothy he is a prisoner and the end is rapidly approaching. Apparently writing from Rome while awaiting execution, Paul is anxious for Timothy to come to him before winter. But more than this, he is concerned that Timothy be exemplary in his life and faithful to the ministry to which he has been called. This final letter of the great apostle is rich and varied. Interwoven are touching appeals, ringing charges, and the note of triumph in the face of imminent death. In fact, Second Timothy is Paul's last will and testament, which, after many years of service for Christ, he closes on a note of quiet confidence and praise to God: "I am already on the point of being sacrificed; the time of my departure has come. I have fought the good fight, I have finished the race, I have kept the faith. Henceforth there is laid up for me the crown of righteousness, which the Lord, the righteous judge, will award to me on that Day, and not only to me but also to all who have loved His appearing. . . . To him be the glory for ever and ever. Amen" (II Tim. 4:6-8, 18).

9

The Pauline Message

The letters of Paul, containing the message of the apostle, were written to meet certain specific situations in particular churches, and are therefore principally pastoral in tone and content. They presuppose the apostle's evangelistic preaching, but give only sporadic glimpses of its nature and data (I Cor. 15:1-11; I Thess. 1:5-10). They also allude in tantalizing fashion to other letters which presumably have not survived (I Cor. 5:9; Col. 4:16), to other visits not recorded (Rom. 15:19; II Cor. 2:1; 12:14; 13:1; Titus 1:5), and to other practices or doctrines never clarified (I Cor. 15:29; II Thess. 2:5-7). In addition, on such matters as the existence and personality of God, the authority of Scripture, and baptism – matters on which there was no dispute within the churches, nor could Paul envision any – there is little treatment except to indicate certain major implications, for these were tenets he assumed were held in common by all believers and elements in the substructure of the faith upon which he believed he could safely base his appeals.

It cannot be assumed, therefore, that the apostle's correspondence as contained in the New Testament reveals the whole of his thinking and preaching regarding Christian faith and practice. Nor is one entitled to treat the collection of his letters as a volume on systematic theology, for though he thought theologically, everything the apostle wrote is set in the context of history and polemic. Nonetheless, sufficient material has been preserved under the direction of the Holy Spirit to allow a fairly clear picture of the main outlines of the apostle's thought. The Christian who looks at Paul's message in its historical setting discovers that the doctrines Paul enunciated and the principles governing his specific exhortations are authoritative for faith and practice today; the same Spirit preserved who first inspired – and it is His also to illuminate and apply.

Originality and Dependence

Paul emphatically asserts that "the gospel which was preached by me" is independent of any human source or agency, having come to him directly "through a revelation of Jesus Christ" (Rom. 16:25, 26; Gal. 1:1, 11, 12; Eph. 3:2-10). His message was so thoroughly his own, in fact, that he refers to it as simply "my gospel" (Rom. 2:16; 16:25; II Tim. 2:8) and "our gospel" (II Cor. 4:3; I Thess. 1:5; II Thess. 2:14). Yet he also insists that his preaching is not radically different from that of the other apostles (I Cor. 15:11; Gal. 2:6-10), and refers in his letters to kerygmatic traditions which he assumes were held in common by all Christians (Rom. 6:17; I Cor. 11:23; 15:3-5; cf. I Cor. 11:2; II Thess. 2:15, 3:6). Indeed, as there is but one Christ there could be only one Gospel. Had it been otherwise, he would have felt he was "running or had run in vain" (Gal. 2:2). Such assertions appear, on the face of it, to be in direct conflict, and have led many to view Pauline theology as either (a) essentially original, being in the main the result of a direct revelation to the apostle, or (b) essentially dependent, stemming for the most part from his Jewish and Christian predecessors – or perhaps as overstatements made in the heat of argument, or possibly even due to later redaction of his letters.

It is a mistake, however, to press such statements beyond their proper limits or to set them in rather wooden opposition one to the other. Paul's gospel given him by revelation was not a gospel differing in kerygmatic content from that of the early Church. Rather, it was a message which included a new understanding of the pattern of redemptive history in these final days, involving the legitimacy of a direct approach to Gentiles and the recognition of the equality of Jew and Gentile before God (Rom. 16:25, 26; Eph. 3:2-10; Col. 1:26, 27). Paul could not claim the usual apostolic qualifications as expressed in John 15:27 and Acts 1:21, 22. He was dependent upon those who were believers before him for much in the Christian tradition, as his letters frankly indicate. But he had been confronted by the exalted Lord, directly commissioned an apostle by Jesus Himself, and given the key to the pattern of redemptive history in the present age. The Jerusalem apostles had the key to many of the prophetic mysteries and were the living canons of the data in the Gospel proclamation, but he had been entrusted with a further aspect of that message which by revelation was uniquely his. Together, they combined to enhance the fullness of the Gospel.

Dominant Perspectives

The key to Pauline theology is to be found in Paul's thought regarding Jesus Christ, and is probably most aptly expressed in the apostle's frequently repeated phrase "in Christ." Paul's theology is Christocentric and his religion a life lived in communion with and response to his exalted Lord. This fact must be maintained in the face of all ethical interpretations of religion – whether Jewish, Stoic or so-called Christian – which lay emphasis upon laws and principles as final criteria. It must also be asserted in opposition to contemporary religious existentialism which seeks to explain Paul's theology along the lines of anthropology. Paul's doctrine of man is only a part of his total thought and subservient to his doctrine of Christ, for in Paul's view, man can be truly understood and life truly authentic only in relation to Jesus Christ. Paul's theology is not even a theology in the narrow sense of that term. While accepting all that the Old Testament teaches about God the Father, Paul's proclamation that "God was in Christ reconciling the world to himself" (II Cor. 5:19) in context indicates that the focus has shifted for Paul from the first to the second Person of the Trinity. Nor can Paul's thought be described principally in terms of soteriology, ecclesiology or eschatology (many people's favorite central concepts to explain early Christian thought). All of these were subjected by the apostle to his overruling and central theme: salvation is salvation "in Christ," the Church exists as the "Body of Christ" because believers are first of all "in Christ," and the future holds promise because history has been anchored and reconstituted at a point of time "in Christ."

Likewise, Paul's thought is predominantly historical, functional and dynamic in nature. It was "when the time had fully come" that "God sent forth his Son" (Gal. 4:4), suggesting that, while metaphysical elements inevitably appear in his preaching, the apostle understood the coming of Christ and the redemption of God in Him first of all in historical terms. And in that God's Son has come "to redeem those who were under the law, so that we might receive adoption as sons" (Gal. 4:5) and "God was in Christ reconciling the world to himself" (II Cor. 5:19), the conclusion is inescapable that the focus of Paul's preaching was on the redemptive significance of Christ's work.

Functional and ontological categories can never be detached or held in isolation from one another, for what Christ did has its basis in who He was and is. Indeed, both are constantly interwoven in the apostle's correspondence. Yet Paul seems to have laid primarily emphasis upon the functional aspect and assumed for the most part (at least in his pastoral letters) the ontological. Only where his message was challenged by some alien metaphysical system that would depreciate the person of Jesus Christ, as happened at Colosse, did he enter into something of an extended description of Christ's divine being or essence (Col. 1:15-19; 2: 9, 10); though even here his purpose in such a description was to clear the way for the proclamation of Christ's redemptive work (Col. 1:20-23; 2:11-15). As his Christian faith came to birth not through metaphysical speculation nor philosophic induction, but resulted from confrontation by the risen and exalted Christ, so he proclaimed the activity of God in Christ as set in a dynamic and redemptive context; though since his preaching had an inevitable metaphysical and ontological basis – and as he was providentially led to a fuller explication of his Christian convictions – these factors inevitably appear in the warp and woof of his theology.

Man's State and Need

As a backdrop to the display of God's grace in Jesus Christ, Paul speaks of man's state and need. In depicting the created state of man, the apostle evidences a qualified anthropological dualism in referring to man as possessing an "inner" and an "external" constitution (Rom. 7:22; 8:10; I Cor. 5:5; 6:20; 7:34; II Cor. 7:1; Eph. 3:16). The division of man into two component parts is often said to reflect his debt to Hellenism. It also appears, however, in strictly Hebraic contexts (Gen. 2:7; 35:18; I Kings 17:22; Lev. Rabbah 34:3; BT Sanhedrin 91a, b). But while acknowledging a structural dichotomy, Paul also insists upon the fundamental unity of the human personality wherein the structural elements comprise intrinsic parts. Second Corinthians 5:1-4 is instructive in this regard, for here, while accepting the fact of man's inner and external components, the apostle longs for consummation in terms of a perfected union of the two structural aspects – explicitly renouncing any thought of a merely "soulish" redemption and any idea of the separation of material and immaterial as ideal. Paul never thought of the body of man as the tomb of the soul or as corrupting of itself. True, it has become a captive vehicle for evil because of the entrance of sin. Essentially, however, the material and immaterial components of man are both created by God to form one complete human personality, and thus that material constitution (a) may presently enter into communion with God (I Cor. 3:16; 6:15, 19, 20), (b) is a medium through which God can be glorified (Rom. 12:1; I Cor. 6:20; Phil. 1:20), and (c) shall in the future experience more fully divine redemption and fellowship (Rom. 8:23; I Cor. 15:35-50; II Cor. 5:1-5; Phil. 3:21). In addition, Paul spoke of man in terms of a number of functional aspects, behind each of which lay the whole personality (e.g., I Thess. 5:23).

In his synthetic rather than analytic approach to man, and in his explicit anthropological formulations, Paul indicates that his basic thought is rooted in the soil of the Old Testament and orthodox Judaism. He differed from his Jewish heritage more in emphasis than in doctrine, stressing as he does the spiritual (pneumatic) nature of man more than the created (psychic); but that must be credited to his Christian experience and resultant convictions. None of this, however, highlights his teaching on man's most important need; for while man as creature is responsible, Paul laid stress on the fact that man as sinner is in rebellion and thus desperately needy.

The Old Testament doctrine of the sinfulness of man was explicated in the Judaism of Paul's day in two ways. The first way stressed the inherited depravity of all men and their resultant personal guilt, and was expressed at least as early as the second century B.C. in Sirach 25:24: "From a woman did sin originate, and because of her we all must die." And it continued through at least the latter part of the first century A.D. in such words as those of Fourth Ezra 7:116-126, wherein the consciousness of personal responsibility is coupled with the cry: "O Adam, what hast thou done? For though it was thou that sinned, the fall was not thine alone, but ours also who are thy descendants!" (cf. 1QH 4. 29, 30; Apoc. Moses 14, 32; II Enoch 30:17; Wisdom 2:23, 24; IV Ezra 3:7, 8, 20-22; II Baruch 48:42, 43).

The other strand of Jewish thought laid emphasis upon a doctrine of good and evil "impulses" *(yetzer)* implanted by God in equal measure within every man, thus de-emphasizing inheritance and attributing guilt to men individually. This teaching can also be found in the centuries immediately prior to Christianity (Sirach 15:14, 15; 1QS column 4), but came to full expression later in Second Baruch 54:19: "Adam is therefore not the cause, save only of his own soul; but each of us has been the Adam of his own soul." This also is expressed in the teaching of Rabbi Akiba in the late first and early second centuries A.D. (BT Sanhedrin 81a). Through Akiba, this teaching became standard doctrine for rabbinic and modern Judaism.

Paul clearly relates man's sin to the transgression of Adam, insisting that through one man sin and death have infected all mankind with disastrous results (Rom. 5:12-21; I Cor. 15:21, 22). He does not, however, merely leave it there, but, like the earlier rabbis, goes on to assert man's personal responsibility as well. There are therefore two emphases in Paul's teaching: a corporate solidarity with Adam by which all men inherit a radical depravity of nature, and an individual responsibility for the expression of that depravity by which all men become guilty (cf. the *krima ex henos eis katakrima* of Rom. 5:16). Or as he puts it in Romans 7: (a) man's history is so irrevocably rooted in Adam that he is forced to cry in effect, "I am in Adam" (vv. 7-13); (b) man's experience is so obviously in opposition to God that he must acknowledge in effect, "Adam is in me" (vv. 14-24); which facts together mean that (c) "I of myself" (that is, man as he now is by nature and practice) am in rebellion against God and unable to please Him (v. 24). Surely man's sin has not taken God by surprise, for Paul insists that the divine salvific plan was conceived by the Creator before the foundation of the world (Eph. 1:4; 3:9), but it is sin which stands as the occasion for the manifestation of God's grace in the person and work of Jesus Christ.

The Law

Paul's teaching regarding the Law is complex, and has been variously evaluated. In the main, two approaches have been followed in interpreting Paul's view of the Law. The first, stemming from Origen and Tertullian, views the apostle as making a distinction between the moral and ceremonial aspects of Mosaic legislation: the moral expressing the eternal will of God for man, which is fixed throughout the course of history and which the apostle considers "holy, just and good"; the ceremonial aspect being a secondary addition to prefigure the person and work of Christ, which symbolism, once finding reality in Jesus of Nazareth, is to be either spiritualized or set aside by the Christian. Often it is claimed, as Origen and Tertullian also asserted, that the absence or presence of the definite article with the word "law" in Paul's writings can aid in determining which usage the apostle had in mind, though not invariably. The second line of interpretation is founded in the exegesis of Chrysostom, Theodore, and Theodoret of the "Antioch School" (though not always consistently), and views Paul's understanding of the Law in more wholistic and historical terms. On this view, (a) the Mosaic law was given not only to express in fuller form the primal will of God for man but also as a developed system of righteousness which would be adequate if man could achieve it; (b) but since man is unable to fulfill the requirements of the Law, its underlying purpose of revealing and condemning sin came to the fore. (c) Christ, however, both bore the condemnation and fulfilled the obligations of the Law (moral and religious), thus providing both redemption and righteousness for all who are His. (d) Therefore, the Christian lives not in relation to the Law but in response to his Lord who has reiterated and heightened the expression of God's eternal principles, borne the curse of the Law, fulfilled the Law's obligations in their contractual form, and enables His own to live lives pleasing to the Father.

The first interpretation became almost universal in the Western church and experienced a revival in late nineteenth-century theology. It appears, however, to rest more on polemic purpose than exegetical principle and to reflect more a static understanding of Pauline thought than an historical. The second underlies to a great extent the Protestant Reformation (cf. Luther's *On the*

Freedom of the Christian), and must be judged to correspond more closely to the thinking of the apostle.

For Paul, then, the Law as expressing God's standard is the inevitable and inviolable expression of a holy and righteous God which has been declared in nature and in the conscience of man (Rom. 1:19, 20; 2:14, 15). It was given at the beginning of human history when man first had need of such knowledge (Rom. 5:14), and was reiterated, clarified, amplified and applied to the people's new situation of nationhood in the Mosaic code. As the Mosaic legislation expressed this aspect of the divine will in the form of concrete regulations, it offered guidance for life and provided a standard for judgment when men fell short. Without denying this aspect of the Law, however, Paul also asserts another function for the Mosaic covenant as well: the Law as a system of works which placed men under a contractual obligation. In this latter sense it (a) came 430 years after the promise had been confirmed with Abraham, and therefore cannot annul such a promise (Gal. 3:17), (b) was added in the process of redemptive history due to the hardness and waywardness of man, and not as a restatement of God's covenant promise given earlier (Gal. 3:18, 19); (c) has its terminus in the coming of God's Messiah (Gal. 3:19); and (d) by its very nature of having been meditated through angelic and human agency reveals itself to be inferior to the unilateral grace of God (Gal. 3:19, 20). Negatively, it prepared for faith in Christ and the reception of the promise by revealing sin to be "sinful beyond measure" (Rom. 7:13; cf. Rom. 3:19, 20). And, on the principle that forbidden fruits are sweetest, it actually stirred up transgressions so that men might understand the extent of their own rebellion against God (Rom. 5:20; cf. Rom. 7:5, 7-11). Positively, it served as a kind of supervising custodian keeping God's chosen people in ward until Christ came (Gal. 3:23-25).

As a system of works given through Moses, the Law came with a valid promise of life and righteousness (Rom. 7:10), but a promise incapable of reception because of the inability of man to fulfill its obligations (Rom. 8:3). It called for complete obedience (Gal. 3:10; 5:3), but in so doing placed men under a curse since men are unable to live up to it (Gal. 3:10). Thus Paul contrasts the experience of men prior to Christ as being "under the law" with the righteousness of God now revealed in Jesus

Christ which is "apart from law" (Rom. 3:19-21; I Cor. 9:20; Gal. 3:23-25; 5:18), and insists that "Christ is the end of the law in its connection with righteousness" (Rom 10:4). In both its negative and positive features, the Law in its contractual form served a vital purpose in the redemptive program of God – and where Christ is yet to be acknowledged, may still function in this manner. It was "counted loss" by Paul only in comparison to the "surpassing worth" of Jesus Christ (II Cor. 3:7-18; Phil. 3: 7-11). Historically, it was given that men might see themselves for what they really are in the sight of God and as a guardian preparing men for faith in Christ. Any return to it for righteousness after the coming of Christ, however, is a return to "weak and beggarly elemental principles" (Gal. 4:3, 9; Col. 2:20), for human depravity prevents man from ever fulfilling its requirements (Rom. 8:3).

The Person and Work of Christ

The central motif in the Pauline message is that the divine plan of redemption has its focal point in human history in the person and work of Jesus Christ. "When the time had fully come," the apostle proclaims, "God sent forth his Son, born of woman, born under the law, to redeem those who were under the law, so that we might receive adoption as sons" (Gal. 4:4, 5).

The work of Christ in Paul's teaching is presented primarily in relation to the Law. In coming "under the law" Christ has taken both the curse and the obligations of the Law upon Himself, bearing both on behalf of those unable to bear either, and thereby reconciling us to the Father. Christ in His death "redeemed us from the curse of the law, having become a curse for us" (Gal. 3:13); was made sin for us "so that in him we might become the righteousness of God" (II Cor. 5:21); "canceled the bond which stood against us with its legal demands, this he set aside, nailing it to the cross" (Col. 2:14); and reconciled us "in his body of flesh by his death, in order to present [us] holy and blameless and irreproachable before him" (Col. 1:22). But the act of Calvary is not the whole story for Paul, important as it is. The apostle does not proclaim a redemption which merely obliterates the curse of the Law, presenting the individual to God as neutral. He also insists that Christ has fulfilled the legal demands of the contractual obligation established in the Mosaic covenant, thus presenting before the Father a positive righteousness for all those who are "in Him."

The thought of the obedience of Christ, although included in that of the sacrifice of Christ (cf. Phil. 2:8), is not exhausted in the consideration of that act. The declared purpose of Jesus included a fulfilling of the Law (Matt. 5:17), and Paul picks up that theme in Romans 5:18, 19, contrasting the disobedience of Adam with the obedience of Christ; for not only was "one man's trespass" countered by "one man's act," but "one man's disobedience" was rectified by "one man's obedience."

This thought seems to be likewise involved in Paul's repeated emphasis on righteousness as based not upon "the works of the law" but upon "the *faithfulness* of Jesus Christ," and given to all who respond to Him by faith (Rom. 3:22; Gal. 2:16; 3:22; Eph. 3:12; Phil. 3:9). That which the contractual obligation of the Law demanded, Christ has provided. He stood for mankind in offering the perfect righteousness, so that all who stand "in Him" stand before the Father not in their own righteousness but robed in His. As James Denney once said: "It is the voice of God, no less than that of the sinner, which says, 'Thou, O Christ, art all I want; more than all in Thee I find.'" And it is because in His sacrifice He redeemed from the curse of the Law *and* by His perfect obedience He fulfilled the obligations of the Law that Paul can assert: "Christ is the end of the law in its connection with righteousness to all who believe" (Rom. 10:4). The sacrifice and the obedience of Christ are corollaries which in Paul's mind could never truly be separated, both validated by His resurrection and living presence.

In his presentation of the person of Christ, Paul has frequently been accused of developing into a divine-man figure one who claimed to be and was originally accepted as only a prophet and eminent teacher. In some areas, of course, development by Paul over that of the earliest Christians is undeniable. In the matter of the titles ascribed to Jesus, however, the situation is quite the reverse, for in this area the apostle is much more limited than were his Christian predecessors. *Christos,* for example, in the Pauline letters, though overtones of its earlier usage still reverberate, usually appears as a proper name, whereas amongst Jewish believers within the Jewish mission of the church it was employed almost exclusively as a title. Likewise such early christological titles as "Son of Man," "Eschatological Mosaic Prophet," "Servant of the Lord," "High Priest," "The Name," "God's Salvation," "Angel of God," "The Righteous One," "Shepherd," and "Lamb of God" are conspicuous by their absence in what we know of Paul, or appear in such veiled fashion that their presence may be debated. Even "Son of God" and "Son" are found less frequently in Paul's writings than in such works as the first gospel, the fourth gospel, and the epistle to the Hebrews; the term "Son of God" appearing only three times in Paul (Rom. 1:4; II Cor. 1:19; Gal. 2:20) and "Son" only twelve times (Rom. 1:3, 9; 5:10; 8:3, 29, 32; I Cor. 1:9; 15:28; Gal. 1:16; 4:4, 6; I Thess. 1:10). By far the predominant title for Jesus in the Pauline letters is that of "Lord," and into it the apostle seems to have compressed most of the nuances of his Christology.

While "Lord" ranged in meaning in the first century from simple respect ("Sir") to reverential worship, it was commonly employed in the Greek Old Testament and the intertestamental writings as a designation for God. And it appears frequently in this manner in the New Testament as well. With this precedent undoubtedly in mind, the earliest Christians ascribed the title to Jesus in their preaching (Acts 2:36), prayers (I Cor. 16: 22, 23), and confessions (Phil. 2:11). Thus it need come as no surprise that Paul proclaimed "Jesus as Lord" (Rom. 10:9), intending by that to designate Jesus as both divine and the object of faith. Probably the Lordship of Christ was first conceptualized by Paul, as well as by the earliest believers generally, within the matrix of primarily religious and historical concerns. Under the pressures of alien ideologies and the need to speak meaningfully to the concerns of the day, however, the metaphysical and ontological overtones inherent in such original convictions were providentially spelled out. Thus in the face of the Colossian heresy, the apostle proclaimed Jesus as the "cosmic Christ" whose Lordship extends over everything that can be envisaged in the universe of God's creation (Col. 1:15-20). And, in view of the rising tide of emperor worship in the eastern regions of the Roman empire, he explicitly identified Jesus as "God" (Rom. 9:5; II Thess. 1:12; Titus 2:13) and "Savior" (Eph. 5:23; Phil. 3:20; II Tim. 1:10; Titus 1:4; 2:13; 3:6; also Acts 13:23).

In Christ

In speaking of the personal appropriation of the work of Christ, the apostle repeatedly employs the expression "in Christ." The phrase, together with its cognates, occurs a total of 172 times in Paul's writings: 164 in the ten letters from Romans through the Prison Epistles (minus the Pastorals), and another eight times in those addressed to Timothy and Titus. It is the major soteriological expression of Paul, being the basis for and incorporating within itself the patristic themes of "victory" and "redemption," the Reformation stress on "justification," the Catholic insistence on "the body," the more modern emphases on "reconciliation" and "salvation," and all the Pauline ethical imperatives and appeals.

Of course, the words "in Christ" can often be understood in Paul's writings to be merely another way of saying "Christian," as, for example, in such a greeting as "to all the saints in Christ Jesus" (Eph. 1:1; Phil. 1:1; Col. 1:2) or in references to "the dead in Christ" (I Thess. 4:16; cf. I Cor. 15:18). And there are a host of passages where the ideas of instrumentality and causality ("by" or "through Christ") or source ("from Christ") could be read into the phrase, and a perfectly intelligible and theologically proper meaning would emerge (cf. Rom. 5:10; 14:14; II Cor. 3:14; Phil. 4:13). But there are other passages where the local and personal flavor is prominent, as, for example, in Philippians 3:8, 9, "that I may gain Christ and be found in him," and Second Corinthians 5:17, "if any one is in Christ, he is a new creation" (cf. Rom. 8:1; II Cor. 5:19; Eph. 1:20). Without asserting a unitary exegesis of the phrase in its every occurrence or denying further implications, it must, therefore, be insisted that in the use of this expression and in his soteriology generally Paul thought first of all in local and personal terms.

Just as the Son is in the Father and the Father in the Son (John 10:38; 14:10, 11, 20; 17:21), and just as mankind is in Adam and Adam in man (Rom. 5:12-21; 7:7-25), without such relationships ever diminishing the concepts of personality and individual responsibility, so Paul, with his all-pervading Christology, speaks of Christ "in us" as man's only hope for present fulfillment and future glory (Col. 1:27) and of being "in Christ" as man's only basis for justification and acceptance. He does not speak of a transference of merit, as though righteousness were a commodity which could be stored or exchanged. Nor does he usually talk in terms of "reckoning" or "imputing," except in Romans 4 and 5:13 where the language is controlled by Psalm 32. Rather, the apostle lays all the emphasis upon a loving response to and personal relationship with Jesus Christ in terms which pass beyond the categories of psychological analysis. Though this may be called a mysticism, it is not the mysticism of absorption, for the "I" and the "Thou" of the relationship retain their identities. It is rather a personal and most intimate communion of man with his God and of God through Christ with man, and is thus the basis for the Christian's life, hope and acceptance.

The Body of Christ

Paul's concept of being "in Christ," however personal, also has a corporate significance, for it means incorporation into a community wherein the members, being intimately related to Jesus Christ, are thereby inextricably related to one another, and are therefore described as the "body of Christ." The expression "the body" as representing the Church comes to the fore in the Pauline correspondence most explicitly in Colossians and Ephesians, appearing in conjunction with the apostle's anti-gnostic polemic in Colossians (Col. 1:18, 24; 2:19; 3:15) and then in a strictly ecclesiological context in Ephesians (Eph. 1:23; 2:16; 4:4, 12, 16; 5:23, 30). Its quasi-technical use in the Prison Epistles, however, is anticipated in the illustration of the body and its members in Romans 12:5 and First Corinthians 12:12-27, in the correlation of the eucharistic bread and the Lord's body in First Corinthians 10:16, 17, and possibly in the words regarding not "discerning the body" of First Corinthians 11:29.

A great deal of debate has surrounded Paul's use of the body imagery. Catholic theology insists that it signifies an ontological reality, thus developing the doctrine of "The Mystical Body" which exists prior to its members and mediates grace. Protestants claim it to be only a metaphor, many heedlessly equating it with some type of "Social Compact Theory" of the Church. The close relation between symbol and reality which is a feature of Hebrew thought in general (wherein symbol and reality are closely joined yet never confused) forbids us to make the identity required in any "realistic" or ontological understanding of the phrase. Yet something, on the other hand, is basically wrong in speaking of Paul's expression as "only a metaphor." Since hearing the words on the road to Damascus, "Saul, Saul, why do you persecute me?" the apostle could never look into the face of a Christian without realizing anew the unity that exists between Christ and His Church.

The Church, then, in Paul's teaching, is composed of individuals vitally related to Jesus Christ and thereby inextricably joined to all others acknowledging a like allegiance. As members of the same body, Christians are (a) to take care not to sin against a brother (I Cor. 8:12); (b) to manifest an attitude of concern for one another, realizing that "if one member suffers all suffer together; if one member is honored, all rejoice together" (I Cor. 12:25, 26); and (c) to recognize that each has been given abilities and responsibilities by God for the harmonious and fruitful extension of the Gospel of Christ, and to get on with the task in a spirit of mutual dependence and unity (Rom. 12:5ff; I Cor. 12:27ff).

It is because of this corporate relationship of believers in Christ that Paul speaks of his fellow Christian as a "brother," a word testifying to the closeness of a believer to other believers and exceeded in the figure of the family only by terms descriptive of the marriage relationship itself – terms normally reserved in biblical language for the relation of the Lord and His people. Similarly, while Paul uses the preposition "in" to signify the believer's personal relation to his Lord, he employs the preposition "with" ofttimes to denote his own unity with other Christians and the believer's corporate relationship within the community. Thus he refers to his brothers "in Christ" as "fellow workers" (Rom. 16:3; Phil. 2:25), "partners" (Phil. 1:7), "fellow servants" (Col. 1:7; 4:7), "fellow soldiers" (Phil. 2:25; Philem. 2), "fellow prisoners" (Rom. 16:7; Col. 4:10), and those with whom he both dies and lives (II Cor. 7:3). All of these expressions have "with" as a prefix in the original Greek.

The Christian Ethic

The Christian life in Paul's teaching is (a) based upon the fact of a new creation "in Christ," (b) directed through the correlation of the "law of Christ" and the "mind of Christ," (c) motivated and conditioned by the "love of Christ," (d) enabled by the "Spirit of Christ," and (e) expressed in a situation of temporal tension between what is already a fact and what has yet to be realized. Although they can be spoken of separately, all these elements must be combined and merged in our consciousness if the apostle's thought is to be rightly understood and the Christian ethic truly exhibited.

As Paul never proclaimed salvation simply by renewal of character, so he never taught the possibility of living the Christian life apart from being "in Christ." It is because the believer is "in Christ," and therefore a "new creation," that life has become transformed (II Cor. 5:17); and it is because Christ is in the believer that Christians can be exhorted to live in obedience to the Spirit of God (Rom. 8:10-14). Apart from this foundation, the superstructure of the Pauline ethic has no rationale or support.

Accepting this union of the believer with Christ as the basic premise, however, Paul goes on to speak of the guidance of the Christian as a matter involving both the "law of Christ" (I Cor. 9:21; Gal. 6:2) and the "mind of Christ" (I Cor. 2:16). By the "law of Christ" he seems to mean not only the teaching of Jesus as the embodiment and true interpretation of the will of God (Rom. 12 - 14; I Cor. 7:10, 11; cf. Acts 21:35; I Tim. 5:18), but also the person of the historical Jesus as the tangible portrayal and example of the divine standard, as is suggested by his phrase "according to Christ" (Rom. 15:5; Col. 2:8) and his frequent appeals to the character of Jesus (Rom. 15:3, 7, 8; I Cor. 11:1; Eph. 5:2, 25ff; Phil. 2:5-11; I Thess. 1:6). This new law of the Messiah abrogates the supervisory prescriptions of the Mosaic covenant for the believer in Christ (Rom. 7:1-6; Gal. 3: 23-26; Eph. 2:15). Nevertheless, at the same time it explicates more fully the divine standard in continuity with that code; and so it is for Paul the external expression of God's eternal principles, setting the bounds for life and indicating the quality and direction which action should take within those bounds. By the "mind of Christ" Paul seems to have reference to the activity of the Spirit enabling the believer to discern the divine will and to form a proper ethical judgment at each given moment (Rom. 12: 2; Phil. 1:10; I Thess. 5:19-22). Without the "mind of Christ," the "law of Christ" remains remote and unattainable. Where the two are in harmony, however, direction is supplied for Christian living.

The "love of Christ" and the "law of Christ" are not so much equated by Paul (as commonly supposed by some, who appeal to Rom. 13:10 and James 2:8) as they are balanced, the latter being one aspect in the directing of the Christian's life and the former spoken of as the motivating and conditioning factor in a life receiving guidance from Christ. That love which motivated and conditioned God's action on behalf of mankind "has been poured into our hearts through the Holy Spirit" (Rom. 5:5), with the result that now love has come to characterize the Christian ethic in the same manner. And as love provides the matrix and context for the ethical life of the believer, so the Spirit provides the dynamic and strength; for the same God who raised Christ Jesus from the dead gives life to our "mortal bodies also through his Spirit" (Rom. 8:11).

All of this is lived out between the polarities of what has been accomplished by the historical achievement of Jesus and what is yet to be fully realized in the consummation of God's redemptive program. In such a temporal tension the believer lives, conscious both of (a) what he is "in Adam," sobering him to the potentialities of his depraved nature, and (b) what he is "in Christ," awakening him to the prospects of present victories and ultimate conquest.

The Consummation of God's Plan

Paul's eschatology, while rooted in the Old Testament and employing the imagery of his day, is basically an extension of his Christology in its distinctive features and focus. God's Son entered the arena of human history "when the time had fully come" (Gal. 4:4), thus inaugurating the Messianic Age and setting in motion a series of events which will reach its climax in the final days. The resurrection of Jesus from the dead and the presence of His Spirit in the lives of believers are the "first fruits" which sanctify the whole redemptive process and give assurance of final consummation (Rom. 8:23; I Cor. 15:20, 23). The declaration regarding Christ's coming again and the believers' being caught up to meet their Lord is based upon "the word of the Lord" (I Thess. 4:15), the essence of which Paul seems to quote in First Thessalonians 4:16, 17. And the apostle's thought regarding the future centers upon the coming again of Christ, the parousia, all else being related to that.

It is frequently asserted that Paul's eschatology underwent something of a transformation during the course of his ministry, maturing from a crude apocalypticism laying all the emphasis upon the future parousia, to a more refined existential understanding which stressed fulfillment in the present and immortality at death. It is instructive to note, however, that the elements which have so often been cited in Paul to evidence such a development appear conjoined rather than contrasted throughout his writings, from the earliest to the last. Thus in his earlier letters, while reminding his converts of the futuristic note in his evangelistic preaching (I Thess. 1:10) and presenting the parousia in imagery strikingly similar to that of Jewish apocalypticism (I Thess. 4:13 - 5:11; II Thess. 2:1-12), the apostle also speaks of Christian conduct as characterized by Christ's living "in" the believer (Gal. 2:20). In writing to Christians at Corinth and Rome, while talking of disembodiment and presence with the Lord at death (II Cor. 5:1-10), Paul also lays heavy emphasis upon full consummation at the parousia (Rom. 8:18-25; I Cor. 15:12-58) and joins in the common prayer of the Church: "Our Lord, come" (I Cor. 16:22; cf. Rev. 22:20). In his letters written during his Roman imprisonment, although speaking repeatedly of being "in Christ" and of the "body of Christ," he also writes that "our commonwealth is in heaven, and from it we await a Savior, the Lord Jesus Christ, who will change our lowly body to be like his glorious body" (Phil. 3:20, 21). And in the Pastoral Epistles, with their stress upon ecclesiastical concerns of the present, there is also the note of "awaiting our blessed hope, the appearing of the glory of our great God and Savior Jesus Christ" (Titus 2:13). Emphases may vary in his letters, depending in large measure upon the situation to which he speaks. And his own expectation of being alive at the time of the parousia may very well have changed during the course of his life (cf. I Thess. 4:15-17; I Cor. 15:51, 52; II Cor. 5:1-10). But throughout his Christian experience and ministry, it was the parousia which held center stage in his thoughts regarding the future.

The parousia in Paul's teaching, then, means first of all permanent union for the Christian with Christ (I Thess. 4:17) and the resurrection of the believer's body, completing the sonship to which the believer has been called by the transformation of that body "to be like his glorious body" (Rom. 8:23; I Cor. 15:

12-58; Phil. 3:21). It also means judgment, though for the Christian the ultimate verdict is already known (Rom. 8:1); whatever else the judgment may mean in terms of purgation and recompense, it cannot affect the salvation of those who have believed in Christ (I Cor. 3:13-15; 5:5; II Cor. 5:10). For those apart from Christ, however, the parousia can mean only "sudden destruction," "wrath," and "condemnation" (I Thess. 1:10b, 5:3, 9a, II Thess. 2:10-12). In addition, at the parousia, (a) "the full number of the Gentiles" will be completed (Rom. 11:25), (b) the promises of God to Israel will be finally fulfilled (Rom. 11: 26-31), (c) the creation will be liberated from the shackles imposed as a result of man's sin (Rom. 8:19-22; cf. I Cor. 7:31b), (d) all rule and authority will be subjected first to the Son and then be delivered by the Son to the Father (I Cor. 15: 24 27), (e) death, the "last enemy," will be destroyed (I Cor. 15:26), and (f) "the Son himself will also be subjected to him who put all things under him, that God may be everything to every one" (I Cor. 15:28).

Though the historical achievement of Jesus is a finished work, its application is progressive and its climax will be reached only in the second coming of Christ. And though the Christian experiences resurrection life and intimacy "in Christ" now, and may know even closer fellowship at death, the full realization of his sonship and the consummation of God's redemptive plan awaits the parousia. For this Paul expectantly waits, joining in the Christian prayer: "Our Lord, come!" (I Cor. 16:22).

10

The Relevance of Paul for Today

The one compelling and inescapable datum of the modern consciousness is its sense of crisis. Men may differ on all other matters, but on this they are agreed. The sense of crisis is the one conviction which the twentieth century seems to have produced. And, tragically, for many it is almost the only conviction which it preserves.

Paul, too, lived in a time of crisis. Like twentieth century man, he stood at the crossroads of cultural, religious and philosophic interaction – and like men today, experienced personally the onrush of competing ideologies and conflicting modes of life. True, many of the express forms of the crises and options he faced must be judged as archaic from the modern perspective. But the underlying issues have remained essentially the same. And to these perennial issues of life and thought the apostle's words and example are as relevant today as they were then, and by the work of the Holy Spirit become guidance for life from God Himself to those who are His own.

His Orientation of Life and Thought

Where is the rationale and goal of life? To what or to whom is one to look for guidance? How is a man to find fulfillment and know meaning in his life? The questions focus on the proper orientation for life, and have been answered in many ways.

Frequently, *propriety* has been offered as the basic principle for life. Ancient codes of jurisprudence, while represented as having been given by a god or gods, stressed almost exclusively civic and social rightness; and modern man usually thinks along the lines of what is proper on the horizontal plane alone. But Paul, in accord with the Hebraic tradition upon which he built, thought first of righteousness and then of rightness, believing that only in the first is there an adequate basis for the second. The concept of *the greatest good* or *the greatest happiness* has served as the foundation of thought and action for many, whether interpreted as the greatest good and happiness for the group as a whole or for the individual himself. But though such thought can be altruistic in motive and noble in expression, "good" and "happiness" have been found to be easily adjustable values when considered alone. And Paul never enthroned such utilitarian goals as the final criteria of life. Neither did he invoke a system of *external legislation* to supervise man's thought and action, as has been the tendency throughout history in an attempt to externalize basic problems and objectify their solutions. Paul knew that man's dilemma lay at the core of life, not on its surface. Therefore he was more concerned with fundamental commitments than with incidental acts, and with the quality of the ends pursued than with the efficiency of the means in pursuing them. Nor was he prepared to assert the Stoic proposal of *inward regulation,* with its dual maxims of "Know thyself" and "Be true to thyself." Man's ego, although created by God, has been taken captive by sin; and even though enlightened, it cannot be counted on either to motivate or to guide life aright.

For Paul, life and thought were theologically and (particularly) christologically oriented. Thus, truth and morality have objective significance as reflections of God's person and nature, and life is lived in communion with the eternal. "For to me," says the apostle, "to live is Christ" (Phil. 1:21). It is being "in Christ" which makes a man "a new creation" (II Cor. 5:17); it is "the love of Christ" which controls him (II Cor. 5:14); and it is seeking to please Christ which motivates the Christian to serve his fellow-men on Christ's behalf (II Cor. 5:9-21). In the person of Jesus Christ, Paul found not only forgiveness for sin and reconciliation with God, but also fulfillment, meaning, purpose, hope, motivation and direction in his life. To a world estranged from God, and thereby lost in a maze of relativity and floundering in the depths of meaninglessness, Paul's clarion call to such a radical reorientation of life is the most relevant message of all.

Sadly, however, most have remained deaf to its appeal because they ignorantly fear the radical reorganization of life involved.

His Treatment of Recurrent Heresies

Paul is also relevant to today's world in his treatment of certain recurrent heresies; for, though his polemical statements were all addressed to specific problems in particular churches or areas during the first century, his words are still to the point as those same errors reappear in more modern dress.

Probably there are few Judaizers, as such, in the Christian church today — at least, few who would argue for circumcision and the strict observance of the Mosaic law as necessary for acceptance by God. But wherever *legalism* is proclaimed as part of the Gospel — whether as certain activities which must be performed in addition to faith in Christ for salvation or certain activities which must be abstained from for complete sanctification — Paul's magnificent manifesto of Christian liberty in the letter to the Galatians, together with his remarks concerning the same issue in Romans and Colossians, continue to carry full force. "For I through the law died to the law," says Paul, "that I might live to God. I have been crucified with Christ; it is no longer I who live, but Christ who lives in me; and the life I now live in the flesh I live by faith in the Son of God, who loved me and gave himself for me. I do not nullify the grace of God; for if justification were through the law, then Christ died to no purpose" (Gal. 2:19-21). "Christ is the end of the law in its connection with righteousness, to every one who has faith" (Rom. 4:10); and because of the work of Christ, God has "canceled the bond which stood against us with its legal demands . . . nailing it to the cross" (Col. 2:14).

Wherever *asceticism* and what might be called *pneumaticism* (the exaltation of certain charismatic powers) are viewed as badges of supra-sanctity, the apostle's words of First Corinthians 7 and 12 - 14 are pertinent. Paul was quite ready to acknowledge that God gives the gift of continence and may well lead a man into an ascetic expression of his faith, and he was never prepared to limit God as to what He could or could not do in regard to the more spectacular gifts of the Spirit. But he insisted that the giving of these gifts was under the Spirit's control, not ours. He refused to accept them as signs of spirituality or as norms of a truly valid Christian experience, lest in the setting up of such standards men are compelled to become slaves to some ideal or to pious men, and not allowed the freedom to be Christ's servants guided by His Spirit. If, in fact, a person is to look for the one mark which identifies the true Christian, the apostle asserted that love must be singled out and considered basic to all other gifts (I Cor. 13). Likewise, the apostle's words in the letter to the Colossians are appropriate wherever various forms of *gnosticism* reassert themselves, whether those forms disparage the supremacy of Christ by their claim for higher truth or nullify the significance of Christ in a person's life by their sectarian system of doctrine. Whatever minimizes the person and work of Christ by its system of philosophic speculation, whether it clothes itself in profundity or piety, is regarded by the apostle as "empty deceit, according to human tradition" (Col. 2:8), "for in him [Christ] the whole fulness of deity dwells bodily, and you have come to fulness of life in him" (Col. 2:9, 10).

All of the above-mentioned heresies (legalism, asceticism, pneumaticism, gnosticism) arise from the human desire to add to the work of Christ. To all of these Paul asserts that fullness of redemption is to be found only in Christ and completeness of life is based only upon Him. On the other hand, *libertinism* minimizes the Lordship of Christ in the life by its renunciation of all external considerations and its anthropocentric insistence on uninhibited expression. While insisting that "for freedom Christ has set us free" and urging his converts to "stand fast therefore, and do not submit again to a yoke of slavery" (Gal. 5:1), Paul also spoke pointedly in that same Galatian letter against a libertine reaction, in the words: "You were called to freedom, brethren; only do not use your freedom as an opportunity for the flesh, but through love be servants of one another" (Gal. 5:13).

Throughout his correspondence with the Christians at Corinth, there reverberate repeated rebukes of such a libertine mentality. To those whose pride in their freedom had made them schismatics, the apostle pointed out that they were really "fleshly" believers and only "behaving like ordinary men" (I Cor. 3:1-4), and urged that they return to the foundation of Christ and the guidance of the Spirit (I Cor. 1:18 - 3:23). Regarding one who thought himself so liberated as to be able to engage in immorality as a spiritual exercise and to despise apostolic correction, Paul says quite bluntly: "Drive out the wicked person from among you" (I Cor. 5:13). To those who would insist as Christians upon their legal rights before heathen courts, the apostle warned that such action would bring the Gospel into disrepute and pleaded instead that his converts be ready to suffer wrong and be defrauded for the sake of the Christian witness rather than engage in such action (I Cor. 6:1-8). And to those who considered themselves knowledgeable in the Christian life, but by flaunting their freedoms were causing other more scrupulous believers to stumble in their faith, he spoke of love as more important than knowledge (I Cor. 8:1ff). Also, he insisted that the Christian is responsible for the welfare of his brother (I Cor. 10:23ff). Libertinism, while asserting the fact of freedom in Christ, fails utterly to realize that its abuse can result in a slavery just as binding as any other (I Cor. 6:12ff), and that freedom also has its responsibilities (I Cor. 10:23ff). In speaking of the nature of the gift of freedom which is in Christ together with the responsibilities involved in the task to which the Christian has committed himself as a new creation in Christ, Paul has spoken pertinently both to those of his day and to us.

His Teaching on Christian Living

In a day when morality is under scrutiny, and new directions in ethics – whether individual, societal or ecclesiastical – are being taken, Christians have need to consider again the message of Paul. Today amid the cries for sanctions and conformity, on the one hand, and the so-called "situational ethics" and relevancy, on the other, the apostle's words strike home with telling force.

Contrary to the humanistic assumption that although human nature is perfectible, it is basically unchangeable, Paul proclaimed that genuine Christian living must be based upon a transformation of character as effected by Christ and energized by the Holy Spirit. Any attempt to live as a Christian apart from being "in Christ" is little more than Stoicism in religious guise. Being "in Christ," the Christian is guided by the words and example of his Lord (the "law of Christ"; cf. I Cor. 9:21; Gal. 6: 2) as explicated and applied by the Spirit (the "mind of Christ"; cf. I Cor. 2:16). In such guidance, there is both the definitiveness of express principles as given by Christ – which incorporate and heighten the will of God as expressed in the Old Testament

– and the situational application to changing circumstances as directed by the Spirit, with the result that the Christian defines his action in terms of both external, eternal principles and internal enlightenment for the particular situation. But being "in Christ" and receiving direction from Christ are not the complete story regarding individual Christian living, important as they are; there are also the matters of motivation and conditioning. And here the apostle speaks of the "love of Christ" (II Cor. 5:14) and the Father's love "poured into our hearts through the Holy Spirit" (Rom. 5:5) as impelling and controlling the believer in all he does, so that the intent of Christ's directions for the believer's life might be properly expressed.

The Christian expresses his Christian ethic, of course, in corporate contexts, for no man lives as an island to himself. Underlying all of Paul's injunctions pertaining to man in his social relationships is the consciousness that while distinctions must necessarily be made in the various and varied functions of men, every individual person, regardless of his station or his task in life, is of great intrinsic worth and the direct object of divine love. This means that in the family, while subjection to one another is enjoined and proper obedience exhorted, love and respect among the individual members are to predominate and bind the family into a viable whole (Eph. 5:21-33). It also means that in the church, while there are differing ministries and differing gifts, all Christians belong to the one body of Christ and are to consider one another in love as equals before God (I Cor. 3:5–4:7; 12:1–14:40) – indeed, to be "with all lowliness and meekness, with patience, forbearing one another in love, eager to maintain the unity of the Spirit in the bond of peace" (Eph. 4:2, 3). And this means that in society generally, while recognizing differences in the various situations in which men find themselves and the various vocations to which they are called (I Cor. 7:17-24), the Christian is to view all men in whatever circumstance through the eyes of redemptive love (Philem. 4-21) and to "do good to all men, and especially to those who are of the household of faith" (Gal. 6:10).

Where this two-sided biblical principle of *equality of persons* and *subordination of functions* is ignored – whether in the family, in the church, or in society at large – there inevitably results a concept of either the inequality of persons or the equality of functions, or both. Humanity, sadly enough, has all too long lived with this perversion of God's order in all of its corporate relationships, and the same errors are being repeated today. To this, however, Paul has much to say in emphasizing the intrinsic worth and essential equality of all persons, while acknowledging the necessary distinctions and inequality of functions existing within any corporate structure.

The Example of His Life and Ministry

A number of times in his letters Paul urges his converts to follow his example. In writing to the Thessalonians, he commended them for imitating the lives of the apostolic band (Paul, Silas and Timothy) and "of the Lord," and in turn becoming examples for other believers in Macedonia and Achaia (I Thess. 1:5ff). In speaking of the problems at Corinth, he urged his converts: "Be imitators of me, as I am of Christ" (I Cor. 4:16; 11:1); and he exhorted the Christians of Philippi: "Join in imitating me, and mark those who live as you have an example in us" (Phil. 3:17). As Paul viewed it, there is a chain of witness and example originating with Christ, mediated through the apostles, and extending out into the world through the succession of converts to Christ. Without minimizing the supremacy of his Lord, he urged an imitation of his own life and ministry.

In many ways Paul stands as almost a unique figure in the annals of Christian history. He combined the fervency of an evangelist, the compassion of a pastor, the perception of a scholar, and the diplomacy of a statesman. He was able to minister meaningfully within the context of their appreciation to Jews in their synagogues (e.g., Acts 13:16-43), to Gentiles having some contact with the teachings of Judaism (e.g., Acts 11:26), and to Gentiles entirely devoid of any Jewish preparatory instruction (e.g., Acts 13:7-12; 17:18-34). He was prepared to correct and instruct his converts by beginning at a point of common agreement, and then leading them on to an appreciation of rightful significance in and proper expression of their Christian faith (e.g., I Cor. 7, 8-10, 12-14). He highly valued his freedom "in Christ" and his rights as an apostle, though he also sought above all else the extension of the Gospel and the salvation of men (I Cor. 9:1-18). In words unable to be improved upon,

Paul gives us in I Corinthians 9:19-23 an insight into his motivations and intentions:

> For though I am free from all men, I have made myself a slave to all, that I might win the more. To the Jews I became as a Jew, in order to win Jews; to those under the law I became as one under the law – though not being myself under the law – that I might win those under the law. To those outside the law I became as one outside the law – not being without law toward God but under the law of Christ – that I might win those outside the law. To the weak I became weak, that I might win the weak. I have become all things to all men, that I might by all means save some. I do it all for the sake of the gospel, that I may share in its blessings.

It has often been devotionally said: "The world has yet to see what God can do with a man wholly committed to Him." Paul was such a man, and the world has witnessed the effect. He possessed a firmness of commitment to his Lord, a fervency of spirit, a compassion of heart, a breadth of outlook, a keenness of perception, and a constant openness to the Spirit. Such an example of a Christian life and ministry stands as both a paradigm and an inspiration to us today.

Bibliography

Amiot, F. *The Key Concepts of St. Paul,* trans. J. Dingle (New York: Herder & Herder, 1962).

Baker, A. E. *St. Paul and his Gospel* (London: Eyre and Spottiswoode, 1940).

Bandstra, A. J. *The Law and the Elements of the World: An Exegetical Study in Aspects of Paul's Teaching* (Kampen: Kok, 1964).

Baird, W. *Paul's Message and Mission* (New York: Abingdon, 1960).

Barclay, W. *Ambassador for Christ* (Edinburgh: Church of Scotland Youth Committee, 1951).

——— *The Mind of St. Paul* (London: Collins, 1958).

Baring-Gould, S. *A Study of St. Paul* (London: Isbister, 1897).

Barth, K. *Christ and Adam,* trans. T. A. Smail (New York: Harper, 1956).

Barrett, C. K. *From First Adam to Last* (New York: Scribner's, 1962).

Baur, F. C. *Paul, His Life and Works,* 2 vols., trans. E. Zeller and A. Menzies (London: Williams & Norgate, 1875).

Best, E. *One Body in Christ* (London: S.P.C.K., 1955).

Bläser, P. P. *Das Gesetz bei Paulus* (Munster: Aschendorff, 1941).

Bonsirven, J. *Exégèse rabbinique et exégèse paulinienne* (Paris: Beauchesne, 1939).

——— *L'Evangile de Paul* (Paris: Beauchesne, 1948).

Bornkamm, G. *Das Ende des Gesetzes* (München: Kaiser, 1952).

——— *Early Christian Experience,* trans. P. L. Hammer (London: SCM Press, 1969).

Bruce, F. F. "Promise and Fulfilment in Paul's Presentation of Jesus," *Promise and Fulfilment* (Essays Presented to S. H. Hooke), ed. F. F. Bruce (Edinburgh: T. & T. Clark, 1963), pp. 36-50.

Brunner, E. "Der Apostel Paulus," *Paulus-Hellas-Oikumene* (Athens: Student Christian Association of Greece, 1951).

Bultmann, R. *Der Stil der paulinischen Predigt und die kynischstoische Diatribe* (Göttingen: Vanderhoeck & Ruprecht, 1910).

——— "Paul," pp. 111-46, "Romans 7 and the Anthropology of Paul," pp. 147-74, "Jesus and Paul," pp. 183-201, "Ignatius and Paul," pp. 267-77, *Existence and Faith,* trans. S. M. Ogden (New York: Meridian Books, 1960).

Caird, G. B. *Principalities and Powers: A Study in Pauline Theology* (Oxford: Clarendon, 1956).

——— "Paul the Apostle," *Dictionary of the Bible,* ed. J. Hastings, rev. ed. by F. C. Grant and H. H. Rowley (New York: Scribner's, 1963), pp. 731-36.

——— "Pauline Theology," *Dictionary of the Bible,* ed. J. Hastings, rev. ed. by F. C. Grant and H. H. Rowley (New York: Scribner's, 1963), pp. 736-42.

Cerfaux, L. *Christ in the Theology of St. Paul,* trans. G. Webb and A. Walker (New York: Herder & Herder, 1959).

——— *The Church in the Theology of St. Paul,* trans. G. Webb and A. Walker (New York: Herder & Herder, 1959).

——— *The Christian in the Theology of St. Paul,* trans. G. Webb and A. Walker (New York: Herder & Herder, 1965).

Chadwick, H. *The Enigma of St. Paul* (London: Athlone Press, 1969).

Chadwick, W. E. *The Pastoral Teaching of St. Paul* (Edinburgh: T. & T. Clark, 1907).

Child, R. L. "St. Paul's Doctrine of Grace and Freedom," *Studies in History and Religion,* ed. E. A. Payne (London: Lutterworth, 1942).

Conybeare, W. J., and Howson, J. S. *The Life and Epistles of St. Paul* (London: Longmans, Green, and Co., 1853).

Dahl, N. A. "Paul and the Church at Corinth According to I Corinthians 1:10 - 4:21," *Christian History and Interpretation: Studies Presented to John Knox,* eds. W. R. Farmer, C. F. D. Moule, and R. R. Niebuhr (Cambridge: University Press, 1967), pp. 337-61.

Dallmann, W. *Paul, Life and Letters* (St. Louis: Concordia, 1929).

Daly, E. J., ed. *Paul, Trumpet of the Spirit* (Paterson, N.J.: St. Anthony Guild Press, 1963).

Daube, D. *The New Testament and Rabbinic Judaism* (London: Athlone Press, 1956).

Davies, W. D. *Torah in the Messianic Age and/or the Age to Come* (Philadelphia: Society of Biblical Literature, 1952).

——— *Paul and Rabbinic Judaism* (London: S.P.C.K., 1955).

——— "Paul and the Dead Sea Scrolls: Flesh and Spirit," *The Scrolls and the New Testament,* ed. K. Stendahl (London: SCM Press, 1956), pp. 157-82.

Dean, J. T. *Saint Paul and Corinth* (London: Lutterworth, 1947).

Deissmann, A. *Die neutestamentliche Formel "in Christo Jesu"* (Marburg: Elwert, 1892).
——— *The Religion of Jesus and the Faith of Paul,* trans. W. E. Wilson (London: Hodder & Stoughton, 1923).
——— *Paul: A Study in Social and Religious History,* trans. W. E. Wilson (London: Hodder & Stoughton, 1926).
Denney, J. "Christianity of Paul," *Jesus and the Gospel* (London: Hodder & Stoughton, 1909), pp. 19-38.
DeWitt, N. W. *St. Paul and Epicurus* (Minneapolis: University Press, 1954).
Dibelius, M. *Die Geisterwelt im Glauben des Paulus* (Göttingen: Vandenhoeck & Ruprecht, 1909).
Dibelius, M. and Kümmel, W. G. *Paul,* trans. F. Clarke (New York: Longmans, Green, 1953).
Dodd, C. H. *The Meaning of Paul for Today* (London: Allen & Unwin, 1920).
——— *The Mind of Paul: A Psychological Approach* (Manchester: John Rylands Library, 1934).
——— *The Mind of Paul: Change and Development* (Manchester: John Rylands Library, 1934).
——— *Gospel and Law* (Cambridge: University Press, 1951).
——— "Ennomos Christou," *Studia Paulina: In Honorem J. de Zwaan,* eds. W. C. van Unnik and G. Sevenster (Haarlem: Bohn, 1953).
Duncan, G. S. *St. Paul's Ephesian Ministry* (London: Hodder & Stoughton, 1929).
Easton, B. S. *The Teaching of St. Paul* (New York: Gorham, 1919).
Edman, I. *The Mind of Paul* (New York: Holt, 1935).
Ellis, E. E. *Paul's Use of the Old Testament* (Edinburgh: Oliver & Boyd, 1957).
——— *Paul and his Recent Interpreters* (Grand Rapids: Eerdmans, 1961).
Enslin, M. S. *The Ethics of Paul* (New York: Harper, 1930).
Farrar, F. W. *The Life and Work of St. Paul* (New York: Dutton, 1880).
Filson, F. V. *St. Paul's Conception of Recompense* (Leipzig: Hinrichs, 1931).
——— "Paul and the Gentile Mission," *Three Crucial Decades* (Richmond, Va.: John Knox Press, 1964), pp. 91-114.
Fitzmyer, J. A. *Pauline Theology, A Brief Sketch* (Englewood Cliffs, N.J.: Prentice-Hall, 1967).
Foakes-Jackson, F. J. *The Life of Saint Paul* (London: Jonathan Cape, 1927).

Furnish, V. P. *Theology and Ethics in Paul* (New York: Abingdon, 1968).

Gaebelein, A. C. *The Prophet St. Paul: The Eschatology of the Apostle to the Gentiles* (London: Pickering & Inglis, 1939).

Gale, H. M. *The Use of Analogy in the Letters of Paul* (Philadelphia: Westminster, 1964).

Gärtner, B. *The Areopagus Speech and Natural Revelation* (Uppsala: Gleerup, 1955).

Gardner, P. *The Religious Experience of Saint Paul* (London: Williams & Norgate, 1913).

Geyser, A. S. "Paul, the Apostolic Decree and the Liberals in Corinth," *Studia Paulina: In Honorem J. de Zwaan*, eds. W. C. van Unnik and G. Sevenster (Haarlem: Bohn, 1953).

Giordani, I. *St. Paul, Apostle and Martyr,* trans. C. Maranzana and P. Williamson (New York: Macmillan, 1946).

Glover, T. R. *Paul of Tarsus* (London: SCM Press, 1925).

Goodspeed, E. J. *Paul* (Philadelphia: Winston, 1947).

Goodwin, F. J. *A Harmony of the Life of St. Paul* (New York: American Tract Society, 1895; Grand Rapids: Baker, 1951 reprint).

Goppelt, L. *Jesus, Paul and Judaism: An Introduction to New Testament Theology,* trans. E. Schroeder (New York: Nelson, 1964).

Grafe, E. *Die paulinische Lehre von Gesetz* (Leipzig: Mohr, 1893).

Greeves, D. *Christ in Me: A Study of the Mind of Christ in Paul* (London: Epworth, 1962).

Hamilton, N. Q. *The Holy Spirit and Eschatology in Paul* (Edinburgh: Oliver & Boyd, 1957).

Harrison, P. N. *The Problem of the Pastoral Epistles* (Oxford: University Press, 1921).

——— *Paulines and Pastorals* (London: Villiers, 1964).

Hatch, W. H. P. *The Pauline Idea of Faith in its Relation to Jewish and Hellenistic Religion* (Cambridge, Mass.: Harvard University Press, 1917).

——— "The Pauline Idea of Forgiveness," *Studies in Early Christianity,* ed. S. J. Case (New York: Century, 1928).

Hawkins, R. M. *The Recovery of the Historical Paul* (Nashville: Vanderbilt University Press, 1943).

Headlam, A. C. *St. Paul and Christianity* (London: Murray, 1913).

Helzner, J. *Paulus* (Freiburg: Herder & Herder, 1964).

Howson, J. P. *The Character of St. Paul* (New York: Dodd and Mead, n.d.).

Hunter, A. M. *Paul and his Predecessors* (London: SCM Press, 1961).

——— *Interpreting Paul's Gospel* (London: SCM Press, 1954).

Hurd, J. C., Jr. *The Origin of First Corinthians* (New York: Seabury Press, 1965).

——— "Pauline Chronology and Pauline Theology," *Christian History and Interpretation: Studies Presented to John Knox,* eds. W. R. Farmer, C. F. D. Moule, and R. R. Niebuhr (Cambridge: University Press, 1967), pp. 225-48.

Jeremias, J. "Paulus als Hillelit," *Neotestamentica et Semitica* (Studies in honor of Matthew Black), eds. E. E. Ellis and M. Wilcox (Edinburgh: T. & T. Clark, 1969), pp. 88-94.

Kennedy, H. A. A. *St. Paul's Conceptions of the Last Things* (London: Hodder & Stoughton, 1904).

——— *St. Paul and the Mystery-Religions* (London: Hodder & Stoughton, 1919).

——— *The Theology of the Epistles* (London: Duckworth, 1919).

Kepler, T. S., ed. *Contemporary Thinking about Paul, An Anthology* (New York: Abingdon-Cokesbury, 1950).

Kinsey, R. S. *With Paul in Greece* (Nashville: Parthenon, 1957).

Klausner, J. *From Jesus to Paul,* trans. W. F. Stinespring (New York: Macmillan, 1943).

Knight, G. A. F. *Law and Grace* (London: SCM Press, 1962).

Knowling, R. J. *The Testimony of St. Paul to Christ, Viewed in Some of its Aspects* (London: Hodder & Stoughton, 1905).

Knox, J. *Chapters in the Life of Paul* (Nashville: Abingdon-Cokesbury, 1950).

Knox, R. A. *St. Paul's Gospel* (New York: Sheed & Ward, 1950).

Knox, W. L. *St. Paul and the Church of Jerusalem* (Cambridge: University Press, 1925).

——— *St. Paul* (Edinburgh: Davies, 1932).

——— *St. Paul and the Church of the Gentiles* (Cambridge: University Press, 1939).

——— *Some Hellenistic Elements in Primitive Christianity* (London: Oxford University Press, 1944).

Kohler, K. "Saul of Tarsus," *The Jewish Encyclopedia,* 12 vols., ed. I. Singer (New York: Funk & Wagnalls, 1901 ff.), VI, 79-87.

Kraeling, E. G. *I Have Kept the Faith: The Life of the Apostle Paul* (New York: Rand McNally, 1965).

Kuist, H. T. *The Pedagogy of St. Paul* (New York: Doran, 1925).

Kümmel, W. G. *Römer 7 und die Bekehrung des Paulus* (Leipzig: Hinrichs, 1928).

——— *Man in the New Testament,* trans. J. J. Vincent (London: Epworth, 1963), pp. 38-71.

Ladd, G. E. "Paul and the Law," *Soli Deo Gloria: In Honor of William Childs Robinson* (Grand Rapids: Eerdmans, 1968), pp. 50-67.

Lake, K. *The Earlier Epistles of St. Paul* (London: Rivingtons, 1911).

——— *Paul: His Heritage and Legacy* (London: Christophers, 1934).

Lampe, G. W. H. "Church Discipline and the Interpretation of the Epistles to the Corinthians," *Christian History and Interpretation: Studies Presented to John Knox,* eds. W. R. Farmer, C. F. D. Moule, and R. R. Niebuhr (Cambridge: University Press, 1967), pp. 337-61.

Leavell, R. C. *The Apostle Paul: Christ's Supreme Trophy* (Grand Rapids: Baker, 1963).

Ljungman, H. *Das Gesetz Erfullen* (Lund: Gleerup, 1954).

——— *Pistis: A Study of its Presuppositions and its Meaning in Pauline Use,* translated (Lund: Gleerup, 1964).

Lohmeyer, E. *Grundlagen der paulinischen Theologie* (Tübingen: Mohr, 1928).

Longenecker, R. N. *Paul, Apostle of Liberty* (New York: Harper & Row, 1964).

Lowrie, W. *SS. Peter and Paul in Rome* (London: Oxford University Press, 1940).

Lütgert, W. *Gesetz und Geist* (Gütersloh: Gertelsmann, 1919).

Machen, J. G. *The Origin of Paul's Religion* (London: Hodder & Stoughton, 1921).

MacGregor, W. M. *Christian Freedom* (London: Hodder & Stoughton, 1914).

McNeile, A. H. *St. Paul: His Life, Letters, and Christian Doctrine* (Cambridge: University Press, 1932).

Manson, T. W. "Jesus, Paul, and the Law," *Judaism and Christianity,* Vol. III, ed. E. K. J. Rosenthal (London: Sheldon, 1938).

——— *On Paul and John* (London: SCM Press, 1963).

Martin, I. J. *The Faith of Paul* (New York: Pageant, 1965).

Mary, S. *Pauline and Johannine Mysticism* (London: Darton, Longman & Todd, 1964).

Maycock, F. H., ed. *Christianity according to St. Paul* (London: Mowbray, 1959).

Metzger, H. *St. Paul's Journeys in the Greek Orient,* trans. S. H. Hooke (New York: Philosophical Library, 1955).

Meyer, F. B. *Paul, A Servant of Jesus Christ* (Grand Rapids: Zondervan, 1953).

Michel, O. *Paulus und seine Bibel* (Gütersloh: Bertelsmann, 1929).

Minear, P. S. *An Introduction to Paul* (New York: Abingdon, 1937).

Moe, O. E. *The Apostle Paul, His Life and His Work,* trans. L. A. Vigness (Minneapolis: Augsburg, 1950).

Moffatt, J. *Paul and Paulinism* (London: Constable, 1910).

Montague, G. T. *Growth in Christ: A Study in Saint Paul's Theology of Progress* (Kirkwood, Mo.: Maryhurst Press, 1961).

Montefiore, C. G. *Judaism and St. Paul* (London: Goschen, 1914).

Morgan, W. *The Religion and Theology of Paul* (Edinburgh: T. & T. Clark, 1917).

Morton, A. Q. and McLeman, J. *Christianity in the Computer Age* (New York: Harper & Row, 1964).

Moule, C. F. D. "Obligation in the Ethic of Paul," *Christian History and Interpretation: Studies Presented to John Knox,* eds. W. R. Farmer, C. F. D. Moule and R. R. Niebuhr (Cambridge: University Press, 1967), pp. 389-406.

Munck, J. *Christus und Israel* (Copenhagen: Munksgaard, 1956).

——— *Paul and the Salvation of Mankind,* trans. F. Clarke (Richmond, Va.: John Knox Press, 1959).

Murphy-O'Conner, J. *Paul on Preaching* (New York: Sheed & Ward, 1964).

Murray, J. *The Imputation of Adam's Sin* (Grand Rapids: Eerdmans, 1959).

Myers, F. W. H. *Saint Paul* (London: Macmillan, 1923).

Nissiotis, A. "Paul as Interpreter of the Old Testament," *Paulus-Hellas-Oikumene* (Athens: Student Christian Association of Greece, 1951).

Nock, A. D. *St. Paul* (New York: Harper, 1938).

Ogg, G. *The Odyssey of Paul: A Chronology* (Old Tappan, N.J.: Revell, 1968).

Parkes, J. *Jesus, Paul and the Jews* (London: SCM Press, 1936).

Peake, A. S. *The Quintessence of Paulinism* (Manchester: University Press, 1918).

——— *Paul and the Jewish Christians* (Manchester: University Press, 1929).

Pfleiderer, O. *Paulinism,* 2 vols. (London: Williams & Norgate, 1877).

Pollock, J. *The Apostle: A Life of Paul* (Garden City, N.Y.: Doubleday, 1969).

Prat, F. *The Theology of Saint Paul,* trans. J. L. Stoddard (Westminster, Md.: Newman, 1926-27).

Rall, H. F. *According to Paul* (New York: Scribner's, 1944).

Ramsay, W. M. *Pauline and Other Studies in Early Christian History* (New York: Doran, 1906).

——— *The Cities of St. Paul, Their Influence on His Life and Thought* (London: Hodder & Stoughton, 1907).

——— *St. Paul the Traveller and the Roman Citizen* (London: Hodder & Stoughton, 1908).

——— *The Teaching of Paul in Terms of the Present Day* (London: Hodder & Stoughton, 1913).

Raven, C. E. *St. Paul and the Gospel of Jesus* (London: SCM Press, 1961).

Reicke, B. "Der geschichtliche Hintergrund des Apostelkonzils und der Antiochia-Episode," *Studia Paulina,* eds. W. C. van, Unnik and G. Sevenster (Haarlem: Bohn, 1953).

Renan, E. *Saint Paul* (Bk. III of *The History of the Origins of Christianity),* translated (London: Mathieson, n.d.).

Ridderbos, H. *Paul and Jesus,* trans. D. H. Freeman (Philadelphia: Presbyterian and Reformed, 1958).

Riddle, D. W. *Paul, Man of Conflict* (Chicago: University of Chicago Press).

Robertson, A. T. *Epochs in the Life of Paul* (New York: Scribner's, 1909).

Robinson, B. W. *The Life of Paul* (Chicago: University of Chicago Press, 1931).

Robinson, J. A. T. *The Body* (London: SCM Press, 1957).

Rolston, H. *Consider Paul, Apostle of Jesus Christ* (Richmond, Va.: John Knox Press, 1951).

Rostron, S. N. *The Christology of St. Paul* (New York: Revell, 1915).

Sabatier, A. *The Apostle Paul,* trans. A. M. Hellier (London: Hodder & Stoughton, 1906).

Sandmel, S. *The Genius of Paul* (New York: Farrar, Straus & Cudahy, 1958).

Sanday, W. "Paul," *A Dictionary of Christ and the Gospels,* 2 vols., ed. J. Hastings (New York: Scribner's, 1899), II, 886-92.

Schep, J. A. *The Nature of the Resurrection Body* (Grand Rapids: Eerdmans, 1964).

Schlier, H. *Principalities and Powers in the New Testament,* translated (Edinburgh-London: Nelson, 1961).

Schmithals, W. *Paul and James,* trans. D. M. Barton (London: SCM Press, 1965).

Schnackenburg, R. *Baptism in the Thought of St. Paul,* trans. G. R. Beasley-Murray (New York: Herder & Herder, 1964).

Schoeps, H. J. *Paul: The Theology of the Apostle in the Light of Jewish Religious History,* trans. H. Knight (Philadelphia: Westminster, 1961).

Schonfield, H. J. *The Jew of Tarsus, An Unorthodox Portrait of Paul* (New York: Macmillan, 1947).

Schweitzer, A. *Paul and his Interpreters,* trans. W. Montgomery (London: Black, 1912).

——— *The Mysticism of Paul the Apostle,* trans. W. Montgomery (London: Black, 1931).

Scott, C. A. A. *Christianity According to St. Paul* (Cambridge: University Press, 1927).

——— *Saint Paul, the Man and the Teacher* (Cambridge: University Press, 1936).

Selby, D. J. *Toward the Understanding of St. Paul* (Englewood Cliffs, N.J.: Prentice-Hall, 1962).

Sevenster, J. N. *Paul and Seneca* (Leiden: Brill, 1961).

Shedd, R. P. *Man in Community: A Study of St. Paul's Application of Old Testament and Early Jewish Conceptions of Human Solidarity* (Grand Rapids: Eerdmans, 1964).

Smith, D. *The Life and Letters of St. Paul* (New York: Doran, 1920).

Smyth, J. P. *The Story of St. Paul's Life and Letters* (London: Sampson Low, Marston, n.d.).

Speer, R. E. *Studies of the Man Paul* (New York: Revell, 1900).

Stacey, W. D. *The Pauline View of Man* (London: Macmillan, 1956).

Stalker, J. *The Life of St. Paul* (New York: Revell, 1912).

Stevens, G. B. *The Pauline Theology* (London: Dickenson, 1892).

——— *The Messages of Paul* (New York: Scribner's, 1900).

Stewart, J. S. *A Man in Christ* (London: Hodder & Stoughton, 1935).

Stonehouse, N. B. *Paul Before the Areopagus* (Grand Rapids: Eerdmans, 1957).

Strachen, R. H. *The Individuality of Saint Paul* (London: Clarke, 1916).

Thackeray, H. St.J. *The Relation of St. Paul to Contemporary Jewish Thought* (London: Macmillan, 1900).

Tresmontant, C. *Saint Paul and the Mystery of Christ,* trans. D. Attwater (New York: Harper, 1957).

Urbel, J. P. de *Saint Paul, the Apostle of the Gentiles,* trans. P. Barrett (London: Elek, 1958).

Van Unnik, W. C. *Tarsus or Jerusalem: The City of Paul's Youth,* trans. G. Ogg (London: Epworth, 1962).

Von Allmen, J. J. *Pauline Teaching on Marriage,* translated (London: Faith Press, 1963).

Von Loewenich, W. *Paul, His Life and Work,* trans. G. E. Harris (Edinburgh: Oliver & Boyd, 1960).

Vos, G. *The Pauline Eschatology* (Grand Rapids: Eerdmans, 1961).

Weiss, J. *Paul and Jesus,* trans. H. J. Chaytor (New York: Harper, 1909).

——— *Die christliche Freiheit nach der Verkündigung des Apostels Paulus* (Göttingen: Vanderhoeck & Ruprecht, 1902).

White, E. *Saint Paul, the Man and his Mind: A Psychological Assessment* (London: Marshall, Morgan & Scott, 1958).

White, R. E. O. *Apostle Extraordinary: A Modern Portrait of St. Paul* (Grand Rapids: Eerdmans, 1962).

Whiteley, D. E. H. *The Theology of St. Paul* (Philadelphia: Fortress, 1964).

Wikenhauser, A. *Pauline Mysticism: Christ in the Mystical Teaching of St. Paul,* trans. J. Cunningham (Freiburg: Herder & Herder, 1960).

Wiles, M. F. *The Divine Apostle: The Interpretation of St. Paul's Epistles in the Early Church* (Cambridge: University Press, 1967).

Wilson, T. W. *St. Paul and Paganism* (Edinburgh: T. & T. Clark, 1927).

Wood, C. T. *The Life, Letters, and Religion of St. Paul* (Edinburgh: T. & T. Clark, 1925).

Wrede, W. *Paul,* trans. E. Lummis (London: Green, 1907).

Index of References

I. Old Testament

II. Intertestamental Writings

III. Dead Sea Scrolls

IV. Classical Authors (Greek, Latin, Jewish)

V. Rabbinic Literature

VI. New Testament

VII. Patristic Writings